D

Afternoon

Afternoon

For Women
at the
Heart of Life

Jeanne Hendricks

THOMAS NELSON PUBLISHERS
Nashville

2nd Printing

Library of Congress Cataloging in Publication Data

Hendricks, Jeanne W
    Afternoon.

    Includes bibliographical references.
    1. Women—Religious life. 2. Middle age—Religious life.
    3. Hendricks, Jeanne W.   I. Title.
BV4527.H46   248'.843   79-21339
ISBN 0–8407–4077–8

Table of Contents

Preface

WARNING! This book may be dangerous to your apathy about aging. If you simply ignore middle age, hoping it will go away, it will. Then, with thousands of other downstream drifters, you will slide over the falls and be awash in old age—possibly dependent on agencies, and on advisors with wet ears and sticky fingers.

If you are like me, you are still a new kid on the block. I don't quite feel at home in the over-forty sisterhood even though I have been here for a while. It's a mistake, it seems — I can't be half through living; I've barely gotten started! I have just discovered the first rule of the game.

Rule number 1: God does not want us to live in a mental almshouse. We are to think, to plan, to respond to what He has written.

A little girl brought a broom to her mother and asked, "Mommy, how do you turn this on?" With Bible in hand, I ask the Lord, "How does this work for me?" His answer, like that of the mother: "Get a firm hold on it and start pushing it around to clean up this dirt."

"Thy word is a lamp to my feet, and a light to my path" (Ps. 119:105).

Jeanne Hendricks
Dallas, Texas

1

The Best Is Yet to Come

The third Sunday of every August of my childhood was hot and sticky. Who of my kin could ever forget that annual end-of-the-summer family frolic? Certainly not this skinny, long-legged youngster from Philadelphia who ended the day with sunburn, mosquito bites, and driblets of ice cream on her new sundress. I fought going to sleep, even on Grandma's crisply ironed muslin sheets and goose-down pillow. I might miss my private light show from the jar of fireflies on the bureau, or be taken unaware by some ghoulie that might float down the attic steps into the bedroom.

Family Reunion

"Now run on outside, and git out from underfoot." That was the first order of the day, which was cool and serene in the early morning. The moist shade on the west side of the big white farmhouse was perfect for chasing chickens, chewing cool mint, smelling wild garlic mixed with whiffs of barnyard manure — and listening to voices from the kitchen that would clue me in on when it was time to go back in and lick the chocolate icing bowl.

Only the men went to church this Sunday. On this

special day the women stayed home and did the "fixin' " for the big meal. By the time the sun was hot, Granddad's black Buick touring car would come chugging down the state road, with the preacher in Grandma's usual place in the front seat. "The reverend" was the only non-family member present. His function was to pronounce the invocation before the meal—a combination thanksgiving for the bounty of the food and a request that the Robertson clan would enjoy divine blessing and protection for yet another year. He would then eat dinner with us and "have to leave early."

In the dust behind Granddad one of my uncles was driving the "good truck," which made an annual trek to the Methodist church in town to borrow chairs. The reunion was held in the orchard, a gentle slope dotted with apple trees under which long planks on sawhorses served as tables. Covered with a patchwork of newly pressed tablecloths, they displayed the clan's culinary arts. In no time a collection of cars thumped, wheezed, and steamed along the gravel drive between rows of Grandma's stately hollyhocks. Aunts, uncles, and funny-looking cousins—my sister and I were the only city kids—climbed out and complained about the heat.

" 'Nother hot day, Will," Uncle Harry would say to Granddad.

"Alie, you're a-workin' too hard in there," he'd yell through the screen door. Grandma would nod and keep right on crushing lemon slices in the lemonade pitcher, mixing potato salad, and slicing pies.

"Tell Bertie to put her eats in the shade — it'll be a short spell 'afore we're ready," Grandma would call back through the door.

Learning Who's Who

"Well, that beats me! L-o-o-k who's a'comin!" All heads turned toward the lane as an old Model-A Ford lurched to a halt and the emergency brake was pulled tight.

"Ain't it old Em! Oh, and that's his new wife, too!" Cousin Emery, as I recall, had been a long-time bachelor.

So it was with eyes wide open and ears turned to full volume that I watched my maternal kinfolk congregate. These people and their unspellable names intrigued me. My mother's family had, I thought, a nice, sensible, pronounceable Scotch name: Robertson. But that wasn't true of most of their friends and relatives and the people they talked about—Heltabridle, Segafoos, Devilbiss, Slonaker, Stonesifer, and all the "baughs" (pronounced "ball"): Arbaugh, Harbaugh, Butterbaugh, Stambaugh. My daddy would reminisce about working for a Mr. Catzendafner. The family doctor was Dr. Billingslea. Reifsnider's hardware store calendar hung in the kitchen. There was often a bit of gossip about somebody Zollikoffer (whose name meant "money chest," and who lived up to his name). And then the Baumgardners, Utermahlens, Dayhoffs . . .

Years later I learned that my Scotch forebears had settled in the midst of a Swiss German community. Naturally they had intermarried. Even my mother had married one—Chester Wolfe—from a schoolteaching family.

The format on those Sunday afternoons was always the same. First was the big dinner and then came game time—softball for the men, races for the children, and cleaning up and visiting for the women.

"Well, I never!" some buxom aunt would inevitably say to me. "Child, you're gittin' nearly's big as your mama!" And I would be pulled into the soft folds of an admiring kinswoman, her large arms almost suffocating me.

"Land sakes, Edna, you and Chester sure got you two smart little girls," she would say, brushing aside my damp bangs.

"Have you got a piece to say for us this year?" As she grinned I saw gold teeth and wondered why dentists use gold. "Well, I just thought so. And don't you forget none, now." Brought face-to-face with having to stand on a platform and say a poem, I would wiggle loose, wishing my part were over.

Getting Down to Business

The "program" was undertaken with utmost seriousness, and its format never varied. It began with the minutes from the previous year, the most interesting items being who had married, who had died, and who had not paid his dues. The "entertainment" utilized available talent; our contribution was always reciting poems or singing duets. Skits (for want of a better description) were presented. Then the emcee, usually my great-uncle Jim (who was privately called a "big bag of wind" by my father), awarded prizes to the oldest, the youngest, the newest spouse, and the family coming the farthest (that was *our* moment, for we regularly drove the 150 miles from Philadelphia to this hallowed Maryland spot). Finally, the family tree, a graphic sketch of the clan drawn with india ink on white oilcloth, was displayed and discussed. Closing prayer was offered by my grandfather.

As the sun lowered over the western Catoctin hills, engines cranked up. "Well, we'd best be gettin' along—milkin' time, y'know." One by one the cars would rumble under the big locust trees and out the lower lane by the barn.

Soon all had left except Granddad's family. Mother was the oldest, with three younger brothers. We "women" cleaned up in the house while the men sent Shep the collie to call in the cows for milking and bedded down the livestock. Grandma fed the chickens and geese and checked the garden for any ripe tomatoes. Mother set the big kitchen table for "a light supper." Chicken wings, a dab of potato salad, white cake (because the devil's food was gone), and Aunt Lena's homemade potato chips (now a little soggy) were all mere prelude to the watermelon, which had been down in the well for two days on a rope. With the farm chores done and much to discuss, the women washed dishes while the men churned ice cream. A little helper with big ears could vacuum in an enormous store of impressions.

After ice cream was served in soup bowls, the grown-ups rocked on the front porch and rehashed the day. Sitting on the porch swing, I made more mental notes until the lightning bugs came out and I heard the inevitable call: "Jeanne, it's time you're gettin' to bed." If it was a good day, I might get to take my jar of lights upstairs with me, but sleep was far away. There was much to think about: *I don't care what my cousin Tom says—that red-headed old meanie—I think being a girl is nice. And I am not going to grow up to look like Aunt Effie.*

*Mama says she's always been fat like that. And I hope I
don't ever limp like Aunt Bertie. And I don't ever want to
marry a man who chews tobacco — ugh! One thing I
promise myself—I will never be one of those old, old ladies.
Dear God: I hope it's all right to pray lying in bed, but I just
wanted to ask You that I don't have to be one of those
cranky old ladies. You don't really like them, do You? Or
maybe You do . . .*

Man's Humpback Theory of Life

Almost a half century down the road and many,
many miles from Maryland, I have entered the grandmother era of life. I find that I am still that little girl
asking God to clarify this whole business about getting
older.

I am glad I asked God rather than somebody else,
because I have learned that most people's graph of a life
span looks like a humpbacked camel. Starting with
birth, a person is thought to improve with age until he
reaches some magical zenith at around thirty or forty
years. After that he is considered "over the hill." A
gradual decline takes place. Enjoyment, privilege, and
usefulness atrophy as the end looms into view. Consequently fear, evasion, and retreat set in.

But God's graph line doesn't look like that. His starts
not at birth but at conception, and moves steadily
upward, right off the top of the graph! I like His upward
mobility in my personal life.

How does the humpback theory work? Our fashion
industry is a glaring example. "Youthful styles,"
"young ideas," "turning back the clock"—every effort
is made to avoid the appearance of age. When the
inevitable happens, we do everything in our power to

look in the other direction. We "gently" remove old-sters from our sight, relegating them, often against their wills, to senior citizen homes. These people, who have built everything we have, are sentenced to unimportance and oblivion.

Nothing New

It has always been this way. Ancient Orientals considered it honorable for widows to throw themselves upon the funeral pyres of their husbands. This Hindu practice of suttee persisted into the nineteenth century. James Michener, in *Centennial*, describes the American Indian practice of leaving older widows to starve when the tribe moved on, because it was not economically feasible to take them. Aged women have generally been considered expendable. It is little wonder that the prospect of becoming an older woman is terrifying.

God's View on Growing Old

In sharp contrast, God does not avoid the subject of aging. The Bible includes numerous stories of old people. There is no cover-up—the facts are clear. There are two distinguishing features about these people: (1) they looked for something ahead, and (2) their lifestyles were at variance with their surroundings.

In candid terms God tells it as it is. Moses wrote: "Thou [Lord] hast swept them away like a flood, they fall asleep; in the morning they are like grass which sprouts anew. In the morning it flourishes, and sprouts anew; toward evening it fades, and withers away" (Ps. 90: 5,6). David wrote: "As for man, his days are like grass; as a flower of the field, so he flourishes. When the wind has passed over it, it is no more; and its place acknowledges it no longer" (Ps. 103:15,16).

The grave is not the end. Physical life, God says, is like a sudden whiff of air that blows through and is gone. It seems strong at the time, but has no lasting value. Over that physical life, God repeats again and again, He will implant a life of eternal quality. When that spiritual life energizes the physical life, an inner core takes root and grows. It infuses the physical life with hope, lifting it out of the mire of despair. "But the lovingkindness of the LORD is from everlasting to everlasting on those who fear Him" (Ps.103:17).

Lifting Power

As spiritual perception deepens, it diminishes the importance of fading tangible life. Understanding grows; wisdom expands; hope of eternal life brightens. Death becomes a glorious homegoing without regrets. God does not intend for older women to melt away into nothingness. With age, the inner person becomes greater than the visible outer person.

How does God do this? His plan is accomplished through a network of relationships: family, friends—a giving of oneself to others—and most important, the personal and growing relationship with the Lord Himself.

I intend to approach the subject of aging, especially the psychological and spiritual aspects, as an investigative reporter would. Our medical world has done a creditable job in analyzing the physical changes that occur during life, but there is a "ho-hum" attitude, a what-can-we-do-about-it resignation concerning mental and spiritual questions. Joyce Brothers, for example, who is probably the United States' foremost pop psychologist, wrote:

> In our superbly modern society the emphasis is on youth. . . . Often the pressures of all the psychological and physical changes can result in depression. Depression is a very real illness and must be dealt with by a doctor. The deeper the depression the more urgent it is that we act quickly, but gently, to get medical help. If physical causes . . . are ruled out . . . then psychological counseling should be tried. . . .[1]

Granted, our professionals have helped, but let us not be so naive as to believe that medical or psychological counseling can replace being wanted and needed.

Supernatural Sources

A reporter is only as good as his sources. I intend to draw from heavenly counsel. The timeless wisdom of the Scriptures fits our needs. What the Bible offers drops into place like the missing piece of a jigsaw puzzle. But first, a word of caution. Bible verses cannot be cut out and pasted down to rubber stamp some false premise.

The Philadelphia *Evening Bulletin* carried a sports story with a New York byline about a player who lost his job with the Boise, Idaho, Buckskins. His manager made the decision "the way I make all my decisions on this club. I pray and get instructions from the Bible. I open to a page in the Bible and look and the answer will be there." For this player he found Ezekiel 12:3: "Prepare thee stuff for removing. . . ."[2]

One cannot use God's Holy Word as a rabbit's foot to reinforce passing whims. The psalmist put it in perspective:

> Forever, O LORD, Thy word is settled in heaven. . . . I
> will never forget Thy precepts, for by them Thou hast
> revived me. . . . The unfolding of Thy words gives
> light; it gives understanding to the simple (Ps.
> 119:89,93,130).

It is the infinite Word which directs us; we do not make
plans and hope God will agree with us.

Norman Cousins, eminent writer and philosopher
and former editor of the *Saturday Review of Literature*,
expressed the human need:

> Human beings are losing their faces. They are also
> losing their secrets. . . . Nothing is more universal than
> human fallibility; nothing is more essential than for-
> giveness or absolution.[3]

It seems that during our first forty years we are
constantly learning. But recognizing that we have not
learned enough to cope with the next forty years, what
are we to do? It is clear by now that no human knows all
the answers: trial and error is mostly a process of
ghastly failure. We do not want to become old and
disillusioned. A few seem to tug at their own bootstraps
with some success. Positive thinking is good when
people and health and trusted institutions are intact,
but when these fail, on what can we depend?

Objectives and Obstacles

I was eager to get going in adult life. I'll show everybody how it's done, I thought. Marriage, motherhood,
holding down a job, breezing through educational
institutions — all these would present few problems.
After all, I had the advantage of Christian values, good
health, and I had married a gifted preacher and teacher.
There was no reason not to soar above the sooty

THE BEST IS YET TO COME

everyday world. Who could lose with provisions like that in her lifetime backpack?

The answer is that *I* could. If I trust in any of those "goodies," I am putting my weight on less-than-solid ground. Marriage? I have the best one going, but my beloved husband, with all his talent and love for me, cannot go all the way into death by my side. My children? Although they are part of my inmost being and I love them and their spouses and their offspring with an inexpressible love, they cannot possibly meet my needs—even if I lived under their roofs. My body? My mind? There are (oh, I hate to admit it) signs of deterioration.

The Future Rests in the Past

Life is full. Each new day is a fresh beginning, but that is only in small part due to what this world gives me. The decision I made as a child—a very simple and humble "I do" which I said to God before I ever signed a marriage contract or was anybody other than the second girl in an unknown family—that response to God's invitation to join His family is the one that counts. One day I spoke to Him in prayer. "Dear Lord," I said, "I got Your message. You said You loved me and to prove it You sent Your Son, Jesus Christ, to die for my sin. When His blood ran out there on the cross it covered all the wrong in my life, and in the whole world, because He was perfect. And You saw it, and You were satisfied. I will receive Your Son as my Savior."

That decision revolutionized my life. He gave me His power, the power that raised Him from the grave and that overcomes everything—*everything*. That decision gave me a clean feeling on the inside, and it goes right on putting a glow on every single year of life. God is watching over me, waiting for me to get through this obstacle course, ready to say, "Well done; now come on Home, and let's spend forever together."

Well, scanning the rest of the obstacle course, I can tell it's going to be an uphill climb. It's been uphill all the way, you know. The high country is rugged, but it does have some beautiful scenery.

2

The High Cost of Loving

The gingham dog and the calico cat
   Side by side on the table sat
'Twas half past twelve and what do you think?
   Not one nor 'tother had slept a wink.
The old Dutch clock and the Chinese plate
   Appeared to know as sure as fate
There was going to be a terrible spat.
   I wasn't there; I simply state
What was told to me by the Chinese plate.

So begins one of my favorite childhood poems. I do
not know whether Eugene Fields intended it to be an
allegory, but as my memory replays the lines depicting
a dramatic domestic scene, I think I see a middle-aged
married couple. In their private world there are fre-
quent storms, but only those who are close to them
watch and fear the inevitable.

Next morning where the two had sat
   They found no trace of dog or cat.
And some folks think until this day
   That burglars stole that pair away.
But the truth about that cat and pup is this—
   They ate each other up.
Now what do you really think of that?
   The old Dutch clock it told me so,
And that is how I came to know.

"They ate each other up." That is precisely what is happening in thousands of homes. Two non-persons coexist and hate every minute. Long before Fields, Paul wrote to the Galatians: "If you bite and devour one another, take care lest you be consumed by one another (Gal. 5:15).

How does that happen? Very recently I met a woman whose husband had deserted her after thirty-two years of marriage. Several years before, he had left her and the children, most of whom were grown, to marry another woman. He brought his new bride back to his former church, asked forgiveness from the elders, and attempted to start a new life. The first wife had found refuge in another church, but she was broken and bitter, wallowing in an understandable but unfortunate self-pity, and worst of all, blaming God.

Mass Murder of Marriages

Marriage is very vulnerable in our society today. Our culture has developed a casual attitude toward the sacred husband-wife relationship. We not only condone divorce, but we also have devalued marriage.

"So what's a piece of paper? A number, illegible signatures, and some hoky official seal," is the opinion of a new-morality woman concerning marriage licenses.

"Yes, I did love him. I meant what I said at the altar. But he's not the same man I married. He's a brute. Why should I go on giving when I get nothing in return? You should live with him!" is the testimony of many older women.

"I tried very hard. We got married; we had kids. We did everything the 'right way.' Now the kids are gone, and we're kidding ourselves — there's nothing there. He doesn't see anything in me, and frankly, I can't stand him. It's not that we hate each other. Don't you see, the spark's gone — if it was ever there. I've had it with him!"

On and on it goes — a hundred different arguments for cutting the cable of middle-aged marriage. For some, it's a sudden wide-eyed realization that there is no ground left beneath the Mr. and Mrs. mailbox. For others, it is simply sticking a label on an ill-fitting connection: *Out of Order.* In whatever way it comes, a howling horde of marital dissidents fight their way toward the exit sign every year.

> Approximately one-fourth of the over one million couples who divorce each year in the United States have been married fifteen years or more. In the last five years divorce among couples married twenty years or more has increased fifty per-cent.[1]

The backdrop and the script may vary, but the curtain comes down on the same tragedy — two people have gnawed each other's spirits from the inside out. Nothing remains but the tombstone over a buried relationship.

Marital Security Patrol

The hounds of husband-wife hassles, a swarm of researchers and counsellors, have set themselves to the task of alleviating pain, from the first choking gasp of a troubled marriage to the final trauma of breakup. A typical commendable effort begins: "Are you feeling strangled in your marriage? . . . We rarely had the opportunity as children to witness a healthy marriage

working. . . ."[2] The idea is to put the blame somewhere
else.

Clear-thinking psychiatrist William Appleton and his
wife, Jane, comment:

> Obviously the bad feeling has to be the fault of a
> particular person, place, or thing . . . a natural out-
> growth of childhood and echoes the litany of adoles-
> cence: "I didn't do it, he did! It's not my fault, it's hers!
> Don't blame me!"

> Divorce is pain. Increasingly easy to say, easy to do,
> according to the overwhelming majority of divorced
> persons, but still a jolting, hideous experience with
> unpleasant and often unexpected consequences. . . .

> Unfortunately, the ideas of mystical change, of growth
> and self-actualization coming out of divorce are fostered
> by the proliferation of simple-minded psychologies in
> practice and in print. The sinister "how to's" with their
> offbeat upbeat promises make everything seem possi-
> ble.[3]

Divorce, whether legal or simply an unratified split,
comes from a shrunken, distorted view of marriage.
Like children playing in the sandbox with Momma's
best china, we have scratched and smudged the exquisite gift of marriage by daubing it with our own mind-
less mudpies.

> "Because of your hardness of heart he wrote you this
> commandment [permitting a man to write a certificate of
> divorce and send his wife away]" (Mark 10:5).

We have forgotten what God made marriage to be.
Jesus reminds us:

> "From the beginning of creation, God made them male
> and female. For this cause a man shall leave his father

and mother, and the two shall become one flesh.' What therefore God has joined together, let no man separate'' (Mark 10:6–9).

Watchdogging our wedlock is pointless unless we begin with the One who made marriage. He is the only One who holds the guarantee that makes it work.

Cleaning Up a Marital Mess

When you are forty years old—more or less—and in the middle of a marital mess, what do you do? Having climbed the road to adult living, it is impossible to go back, and the roadblocks ahead seem impossible to negotiate.

The dissolution of marriage is one of life's most painful, humiliating experiences, and is severely damaging to self-esteem. Robert Weiss, psychiatrist and sociologist at Boston University and Harvard University Medical School, has stated that the divorce process produces incoherence, discord, silence, a new loneliness, money problems (only about one-third of divorcées are well educated), and severe distortion of reality. It takes one year to realize what has happened, two years before a new identity is crystallized, and three to four years before that identity can become operational.[4]

To the Christian woman for whom all human help seems to have evaporated, there comes through the murky smog of her confusion a beam of light, an invitation:

"Come to Me, all who are weary and heavy-laden, and I will give you rest. Take My yoke upon you, and learn from Me, for I am gentle and humble in heart; and you shall find rest for your souls. For my yoke is easy, and My load is light" (Matt. 11:28-30).

This implies there are three essential ingredients for healing of the spirit: (1) Move out of self and into Christ; (2) Give Him the burden and relax—find rest; and (3) Get into the harness with Him and learn from Him.

Marriage as God Intended

Possibly the clearest blueprint of what God wants wives to be is the list of standards Paul wrote to Timothy, his young son in the faith. Church leaders, he said, must be men of high quality. What kind of women are married to these men? His description is what every Christian wife should strive to fit (1 Tim. 3:11):

(1) "Dignified"—This woman is to evoke from others esteem and high regard. Every little girl, it is safe to say, has some woman she wants to be like. Here is God's prototype. Purity, graciousness, and selflessness are an attractive wardrobe that earns respect.

(2) "Not malicious gossips"—Our unruly tongues are like "hot lines," to be used with discretion. Throughout the Bible God warns about detonating this potentially destructive bomb. James waves the red flag, calling an uncontrolled tongue a runaway horse, a rudderless ship, and a forest fire (James 3:3-6).

David said: "Who is the man who desires life, and loves length of days that he may see good? Keep your tongue from evil and your lips from speaking deceit" (Ps. 34:12,13).

"But I'm always saying things I don't mean. I just can't control it," a very talented actress once told me.

"Wait a minute," I said. "When you are up on that

stage saying your lines you are uncommonly gifted at saying anything in just the right way — you have complete control. Now don't tell me you can't help what you say at home."

The malady David described is entirely curable; it is a matter of the will. We are individually responsible for controlling our tongues.

(3) "Temperate" — The idea here is vigilance and sober self-discipline. It is the opposite of drunkenness, wherein a person loses control. We are familiar with the holiday-time warning: "If you drink, don't drive." Driving an automobile demands judgment and a facility for decision-making; it calls for alertness and obedience to traffic laws. It's the same with spiritual temperance. Paul says a wife is to know what's going on and to be able to function and follow rules.

(4) "Faithful in all things"—We have sentimentalized "good old Mom" out of proportion, but at the heart of our sentiment is the conviction that you can count on her. She will love you, no matter what. She won't mislead you; she is reliable. Of course, all mothers do not measure up, but nevertheless God tells us that wives are to be totally dependable.

One woman who fleshes out this trustworthy concept is the "virtuous woman" of Proverbs 31. Her husband, a man of position and worldly accomplishment, "trusts in her" (Prov. 31:11). Trust is earned through performance.

Some years ago my busy husband had despaired of being able to carry out our plans for a family vacation. His schedule had tightened, and we had regretfully concluded that our cherished annual trip to Colorado would have to be canceled. Then, while he was in

California, a sudden change of plans opened up a whole week.

"Honey, guess what!?!" he said over the phone. The good news came, but ten days was not enough time to drive round trip from Texas to Colorado and still have time for a vacation.

"No, but you drive and meet me there." Me? Take four very small children more than eight hundred miles? Overnight in the motel? Meals in restaurants? All without Daddy? I was uneasy. What if the kids became restless and unruly while I was driving? (I tucked a paint paddle under the front seat, just in case.) I strained my brain thinking up "fun things to do" to keep two boys and two girls harmonious and happy in a station wagon on a hot highway.

When we stopped at a service station in the Texas panhandle, the children howled with laughter when a woman looked inside my traveling playpen and drawled, "Oo-o-oh, honey! I know just how you feel. I once had a man walk out and leave me with a passel of young 'uns, too!"

It was an excited junior reception committee that greeted Daddy at the Colorado Springs airport. For me it was a personal victory. My husband had trusted me more than I had trusted myself.

Any wife who wants to can be trustworthy. It isn't a matter of talent or intelligence; it is a matter of integrity —of being true to your word and getting the job done.

Marriage in Motion

Having peeked behind the public image, we detect women who are far off course from the divine gauge of Scripture. We women have generally abandoned our compasses, and we are lost, wandering in a marital maze but finding no familiar landmarks to put us back on course. The milestones are there, however, if we will but look and follow.

God does not expect us to live without asking questions. The Bible is full of answers, but they mean nothing unless we ask. In near-Bohemian style John the Baptist preached repentance in the Judean wilderness. Such unorthodox methods raised questions; God intended that they should. Luke reports that everyone raised his eyebrows: "The multitudes were questioning . . . 'What shall we do?' . . . Some tax-gatherers came also to be baptized, and they said . . . 'Teacher, what shall we do?' . . . Some soldiers were questioning . . . 'What shall we do?' . . . All were wondering in their hearts . . ." (Luke 3:10–15).

This brings us to a question. If God intends loving, harmonious, monogamous marriage to work in the final quarter of the twentieth century, what is the key to keeping the relationship intact? The standards of Scripture have already been examined, but still there are Christian women of high character who know the Word of God, and yet, even such as these find their marriages faltering. Dare we ask God for an explanation?

Before we ask He has already answered. The Book of 1 Peter, written to those who believed in Jesus Christ and followed His teaching, instructs us in how to live in a hostile world.

Submission: Quicksand of Matrimony

Wives are commanded to submit themselves voluntarily to their husbands. This commitment will produce wonders (1 Pet. 3:1). This thumbnail sketch of the post-honeymoon home certainly does not measure up to *Young Homemaker* magazine, but it does help to explain why we're off the track.

More questions now seem in order. (Please notice that the Lord never rebuked His followers for asking questions, only for failing to believe His explanations.) So let us ask Him about submission. Is submission for every woman? Considering some husbands we see, one feels justified in asking the question.

A friend of mine told a story at the lunch table about a saintly believer who suffered under the heavy hand of her brutal, drinking husband. For months he came home and beat her and cursed her. To each affront she responded quietly with a blessing, a word of concern for him, and private prayer. When he staggered home —no matter what the hour—she rose from bed, if need be, greeted him lovingly, and served him a hot meal which she had kept ready. Finally, after more than a year of this response, he came home one day and broke into tears. He apologized and asked her to pray with him to find God for his own life.

"Now there's an example of real submission we can all take a lesson from," my friend concluded, and the other women around the table nodded in affirmation. I sat very still, quietly taking exception.

One of the classic errors of our present Christian world is taking the experience of one person and making it a rule of life for everyone. "Lord," I began to ask, "What is submission, really? I know women who would be crushed beyond salvaging if they were called to live with that situation. And I myself could never quietly allow myself to be beaten by a drunken bum without retaliation. What do You mean by submission?"

Over the years I have been shown pieces of that puzzle. First, a hard look at the command:

> In the same way, you wives, be submissive to your own husbands so that even if any of them are disobedient to the word, they may be won without a word by the behavior of their wives, as they observe your chaste and respectful behavior (1 Pet. 3:1,2).

It is an imperative. God has issued a command to me as a wife. He did not tell me I had to get married, but since I did, I am now in a category to which certain rules apply. What is "in the same way"? Looking back to the previous verses, I see that Jesus Christ is being described: "While being reviled, He did not revile in return; while suffering, He uttered no threats, but kept entrusting Himself to Him who judges righteously" (1 Pet. 2:23). *That* is the way we are to be submissive.

Another question, Lord. "Jesus, Your Son, was God in human form. I could never do what He did, could I? Then I remember the Sermon on the Mount: "Love your enemies, bless them which persecute you. . . forgive. . . ." They are all commands which require the exercise of my will.

It still doesn't make sense, but back to the husbands. "Be submissive to your husbands." Three observations surface immediately. Submission is *voluntary*; I have to do it on my own; it is not imposed, nor does it come naturally. It is a *strong* command, using a reflexive verb that has its root meaning in military terminology, literally "to rank under." I am told to rank myself under my husband. And this does not apply to another husband, just *my own*, the one God gave me.

The attitude of submission has a specific purpose—to change an unbelieving husband to a believer in God's Word. And it is all to be done "without a word." It is reminiscent of Joshua's quiet march around the city of Jericho day after day. You would never find that strategy in the military manuals, but God ordered it. So also it is with marriage and submission.

The secret, Peter said, is the "behavior of their wives." Husbands will see purity and reverence. Then Peter explained that the beauty is not on the outside, but in "the hidden person of the heart, with the imperishable quality of a gentle and quiet spirit, which is precious in the sight of God" (1 Pet. 3:4).

The idea of inner beauty is nothing new. For generations preachers have been exhorting women in this. But what we have done so often is to fake it. We women have learned to keep our mouths shut, thus appearing quiet and gentle on the outside, while inside we are raging torrents. And we have called that submission.

That calm-exterior/boiling-interior combination is simply a tempest in a teapot. Better to contain it than to splatter it all over, but that is not true submission. Submission is active, but how do you get it in gear?

The sister command (Eph. 5:22) tells us to submit "as to the Lord." Earlier we saw in 1 Peter that we are to imitate Jesus Christ; now we are to use our personal relationship to Him as a pattern for the husband-wife relationship. Clearly, we are in over our heads. There's not a husband in a carload who deserves that kind of treatment. And therein lies the secret. We must employ supernatural dynamics.

Submit — with a serene spirit: "I can do all things through Him who strengthens me" (Phil. 4:13). It is said of Sarah Edwards (Jonathon's wife): "Her character became his proof that the distant God of his speculations was also a tender personal God who moves about in the midst of human affairs. In the last moment of

Edwards' life he did not speak about theology. He spoke of Sarah and their 'uncommon union.' "[5]

One more question: Why wives? Throughout the New Testament God repeatedly picks up His pointer and touches "wives" when He talks about submission. He does mention generally that Christians are to submit to one another in love, but why the accent on wives? Peter hints at a logical explanation: "For such is the will of God that by doing right you may silence the ignorance of foolish men" (1 Pet. 2:15). Since a wife's submission to her husband is an *unnatural* response, those who witness it will "observe them [your good deeds] and glorify God" (1 Pet. 2:12).

But what if a wife consistently submits to her husband and he continues to mistreat her? Peter answers: "Who is there to harm you if you prove zealous for what is good? But even if you should suffer for the sake of righteousness, you are blessed" (1 Pet. 3:13). "If when you do what is right and suffer for it you patiently endure it, this finds favor with God" (1 Pet. 2:20). Now it is beginning to make sense; submission to my husband is possible, even joyful, because I take each decision and give it to the Lord. I'm looking for His blessing and commendation more than my husband's.

Of all gems, diamonds are the most brilliant. How are they polished? "Two diamonds are . . . rubbed one against the other until the irregularities are ground away. . . . diamond powder . . . comes into use as the only material for polishing."[6] What a beautiful picture of God's polishing process of husbands and wives. He crushes the rough edges that jut out of our lives and uses them to bring out the luster, so that marriage will show to the world a multi-faceted reflection of His Person in our lives.

3
Grad School for Parents

I turned my car from the busy street into the quiet drive of the memorial park, stopped under the arms of a bare oak tree, and climbed the winding stone steps toward tall, carved doors.

"May I help you, Ma'am?" inquired the pleasant but serious woman behind the information desk.

"Yes, please. I need to see a funeral director," I responded. She pressed a button, spoke to someone, and smiled.

"He will be here in just one moment." I unbuttoned my heavy coat and looked around the tastefully designed alcoves of the large reception room. A group of family members quietly occupied one section by a window. The pale winter sun reflected wet eyes and uneasy faces.

"Mrs. Hendricks?" A vibrant male voice turned me around. I followed him to an office with comfortable chairs and sample grave markers displayed on the shelf. "Now, how may I help you?"

"I need to make arrangements for . . . for a graveside service . . . for a stillborn infant," I replied in a low, halting voice. With dispatch he pulled out papers, posed questions, and asked for signatures. I mentally trotted along with him like a puppy dog in unfamiliar territory.

"And what relation are you to the deceased?"

"I—ah—I'm the maternal grandmother." My very first duty as a new grandmother was to make funeral arrangements.

I moved in a daze . . . to the hospital and a grieving daughter . . . to the waiting but never-to-be-used nursery where layette items were chosen for burial clothes . . . back to the cemetery . . . back to the hospital . . . comfort . . . hug . . . pray . . . talk . . . to the doctor . . . talk on the phone . . . try to explain . . . nights of hurting . . . days of helping . . . back to the cemetery and the bitter January wind . . . looking for the last time at the tiny blue gingham box with the shivering flowers in the icy January blast. "Though I walk through the valley of the shadow of death . . ."

"Lord," I reflected on my pillow that night, "it was not that many years ago when my first child, this crushed and confused daughter of mine, came very close to being another casualty. She was an eager, willful little creature who could not wait a full nine months to grow. She fought her way out to an unfriendly world, just barely winning that first battle with breathing — skinny, bluish, screaming, they told me. You let her live, Lord. You gave me my firstborn child in good health, but You took her firstborn away. I don't understand, Lord, but You know best."

Loving and Learning

Death and life are both part of the huge complex of parenthood. Possibly the deepest discernment that comes as one stands on the pinnacle of the mid-century

mark is an awe of the right to life. Being a mother —
shivering at the mystery of a new life coming from my
body, or shuddering with helpless dread at the ease
with which a new life leaves so quickly — demands a
mulish love.

Motherhood does not go away. The up-and-down,
in-and-out pattern of life cannot erase the awareness
that I have borne a child. I will never be the same again
because of the change in my love-ability. Were I to add
personally to my survey of American women, I would
answer the question, "What do you want to be remembered for?" with this response: "I would like it said of
me in the coming generation: 'Grandma? I hear she was
a very tenacious person. She never gave up loving —
either God or people. When her heart got a handle on
you, even though you didn't see her much, you knew
she loved you and was praying for you.' "

Many of us have become "older and wiser." As
women have for centuries, we blundered our way
through the experience of having children, comforted
to know now from modern research that many of our
instincts were "just what the doctor ordered."

Without even being aware of it, the overwhelming
majority of women cradle their infants in the left arm,
regardless of their particular handedness, where the
infant can hear and be soothed by the maternal
heartbeat familiar from uterine life.

Close-up films of women after childbirth show a common sequence of approaches when their nude babies
are placed at their side. They touch its fingers and toes
with their own fingertips, put the palm of their hand on
the baby's trunk, then enclose the infant with their
arms, all the while rotating their heads to an *en face*
position to achieve full parallel eye contact, with increas-

ing tension in the mother until her baby's eyes are open and the eye contact is made.[1]

Did I do that? I'm sure I did. Now, knowing it is standard procedure, how exciting it is to watch young mothers follow a built-in maternal care plan. Being a mother means falling into step with a much higher and broader pattern than most of us realize.

The sweet and spicy sayings of latter-day sages serve only to soothe the feelings and focus on the obvious. Beyond man's shortsighted description of living are God's endless boundaries:

> O LORD, Thou has searched me and known me. . . . Where can I go from Thy Spirit? Or where can I flee from Thy presence? If I ascend to heaven, Thou art there; if I make my bed in Sheol, behold, Thou art there. If I take the wings of the dawn, if I dwell in the remotest part of the sea, even there Thy hand will lead me, and Thy right hand will lay hold of me. . . . For Thou didst form my inward parts; Thou didst weave me in my mother's womb. I will give thanks to Thee, for I am fearfully and wonderfully made; wonderful are Thy works, and my soul knows it very well. My frame was not hidden from Thee, when I was made in secret. . . . Thine eyes have seen my unformed substance; and in Thy book they were all written, the days that were ordained for me, when as yet there was not one of them . . . (Ps. 139).

Pass It On

Since God had a plan for our lives before they began, then the only rational procedure is to follow His instructions for living. A mother named Jochabed did just that. It was a ragtag group of newly emancipated slaves who followed Moses through a desert wilderness, who threw a collective temper tantrum when they got tired of manna, and who declared a sit-down strike when it was time to band together and take over their new territory.

Still, God patiently fed them and nursed them, and at last they were on the verge of marching in to the promised land of Canaan. Moses' farewell talk addressed variations on an urgent theme: "Don't forget." Over and over the wise old prophet, whose memory spanned battles from Egypt to Canaan, warned the young generation, ". . . in order that you may live and go in and take possession of the land. . . . your wisdom and understanding . . . only give heed to yourself and keep your soul diligently, lest you forget . . . *make them known to your sons and your grandsons"* (Deut. 4:1–9, italics mine).

We are to live, Moses said, with a three-generation perspective. As children, we know our parents and usually our grandparents. As adults, we shift to the middle position, our parents before us and our children after us. As years progress we become grandparents, influencing our children and our grandchildren. This is the triple responsibility the Bible presents. God does not leave us in doubt; the alternatives are clear:

> "When you become the father of children and children's children and have remained long in the land, and act corruptly, and make an idol in the form of anything, and do that which is evil in the sight of the LORD your God . . . you shall surely perish quickly. . . . But from there you will seek the LORD your God, and you will find Him if you search for Him with all your heart and all your soul. . . . For the LORD your God is a compassionate God; He will not fail you nor destroy you nor forget . . ." (Deut. 4:25,26,29–31).

My paternal grandfather came to stay with our family for a long visit shortly before he died. He had been a sometime country schoolteacher in his younger years and the writer of a simple, homespun column in the rural newspaper. He was fascinated by our new set of encyclopedias. I recall that he began at the first volume and read it, word for word, from A to Z. I was probably about twelve or fourteen years old, and although I admired his white beard, I kept my distance because when he kissed me he scratched my face with his whiskers.

One day, however, I came home from school and he asked me to sit down beside him on the sofa.

"Do you ever read these books?" he asked.

"Oh, sometimes, when I have to do an assignment," I replied.

"You should read them just to read," he smiled. "They will help you know what you need to know before you need it. This set of books is better than a bank full of money."

From then on I never walked by the encyclopedias without a twinge of conscience. Sometimes I even picked up one of them and read just for fun. Grandpop was trying to tell me what Moses told the children of Israel: children need to have truth worked into the fiber of their lives early, before critical tests come. Moses had learned that from firsthand experience.

Black Market Baby

Turn back the pages of Moses' diary. His parents, Amram and Jochabed, were locked into Pharaoh's massive Egyptian slave camp. Researchers who have studied slavery tell us that one outstanding characteristic of a slave society is the minimizing of men. With humiliation of their masculinity comes a rise in the influence of women. So it was with the Israelites.

When Pharaoh posed his plan for Hebrew population control, he talked to the midwives, the most important leaders of the people. Finding them uncooperative, he issued a mass-murder decree. Every boy baby born to the Israelites must be thrown into the Nile River.

Jochabed heard and acted. She was, with her husband, a Levite. What did that mean? This godly couple called Jacob their great-grandfather. Levi, his third son, had been born of Leah, that first unwanted, unloved wife of the patriarch who cried out when her firstborn arrived, "Surely now my husband will love me." Then again she conceived and lamented, "Because the LORD has heard that I am unloved, He has therefore given me this son also." In continuing agony her third son, Levi, was born, and she said, "Now this time my husband will become attached to me, because I have borne him three sons" (Gen. 29: 31–34).

The Book of Proverbs declares that "an unloved woman when she gets a husband" is one of the four things that makes the earth tremble (Prov. 30:23). Little wonder, then, that on his deathbed Jacob prophesied of Simeon and Levi: "Their swords are implements of violence. . . . in their anger they slew men, and in their self-will they lamed oxen" (Gen. 49:5,6). Moses sprang of sturdy, aggressive stock.

The historian Josephus reports that Moses was a decorated war hero, having successfully led the Egyptian forces in the south to victory over the Ethiopians. Stephen, the first Christian martyr, recounted in his defense that Moses was "educated in all the learning of the Egyptians, and he was a man of power in words and deeds" (Acts 7:22).

Able, educated, wealthy, and probably heir-apparent—the combination could have been lethal to Jewish emancipation had it not been thwarted by Moses' fiery nature. A spark of indignation flared when he witnessed an Egyptian mistreating a Hebrew. In the heat of anger, he killed the offending Egyptian. Could it possibly have been that Pharaoh held Moses suspect in these matters, anyway, despite his outstanding military and academic record? At any rate, he was wanted for murder and fled for his life.

Return of Distant Memories

Forty long years passed — four decades of herding sheep, the despised occupation of his people in Goshen, the lonely, humble nomadic existence that Moses previously had been spared as a member of the palace elite. His idealistic dreams of delivering his people were now dashed, and his disillusionment was obvious: he had named his first son Gershom ("I am an alien in a foreign land").

Yet when this period of seasoning was over, God kept an appointment. He confronted Moses in a burning bush and delivered His next assignment: Go to Pharaoh and deliver My people

An anguished dialogue followed. Moses was reluctant to return to the scene of his personal disaster, and he had long since attempted to store his early training away permanently.

Having protested in vain to God, Moses packed up his wife and sons and started for Egypt. But on the journey the Lord met him and confronted him with his incomplete obedience. Had he, in deference to his Midianite wife Zipporah, neglected to circumcise his son, as God had commanded all Jews to do? Or had this omission been an act of personal spiritual defection? Whatever the reason, Moses' failure to circumcise his son became a temporary barrier to his performing the assignment in Egypt. The record of Exodus seems to indicate that Zipporah was angry. She herself performed the surgery and, taking her sons, apparently left Moses to return to her father's home (Exod. 4:24–26; cf. 18:2–4).

The most important training of Moses' early life took place not in the sophisticated Egyptian palace, but in the presence of his godly mother. Little wonder that as an old man he counseled his wilderness-weary kinsmen to impress upon their children the commandments of the Lord.

> ". . . talk of them when you sit in your house and when you walk by the way and when you lie down and when you rise up. . . . When your son asks you . . . 'What do the testimonies and the statutes and the judgments mean which the LORD commanded you?' then you shall say . . ." (Deut. 6:7,20).

Parents and grandparents do not exist, as our American experience would suggest, simply to give *things* to children. They exist to give truth — eternal, life-sustaining truth—which God intends to be worked into the young lives touched by their influence.

Loving at a Distance

How can I teach my grandchildren when they are two thousand miles away? Our modern, mobile society cuts deeply into cross-generational contacts. With mobility, however, goes improved communications. A bit of conscientious creativity can be employed. My older son recently celebrated his twenty-ninth birthday, the first one since his maternal grandmother was called home to heaven.

"I really miss getting her card this year," he said. Why? Not because he needed another birthday greeting, but because he wanted that assurance that he had come to depend upon—that he was loved and remembered in prayer by a faithful grandmother.

Books, notes of encouragement, phone calls—there are many ways for a grandparent to love at a distance. It takes effort, but what an investment! Possibly the most valuable provision a grandparent can make is the endowment of concerted prayer.

Standing in bold relief in my memory is my husband's grandmother. When I knew her she was mellowed with age, a gentle white-haired matron, but I am told that in her earlier years she was a stubborn Pennsylvanian Dutch fräulein. One of her passions in life was to see her grandson grow up to be a minister of the gospel. To this end she prayed fervently, insistently. It was her prayers, in fact, spoken aloud because of her hearing problem, that actually melted down her grandson's resistance to God's hand in his life.

She refused to give up, and long after he had moved to Texas and was submerged in his own family life, she was still pleading with God on his behalf. Only eternity will reveal the extent of her intercessory endowment.

Double-Digit Disappointment

Grown children must leave home. I suspect that every mother has wistful twinges. It's a mixture of

triumph and heartache, depending on the circumstances. Says Nathan W. Turner, psychologist:

> . . . it's a familiar story. Husband and wife devote their
> lives to bringing up their children. Then the children
> leave home and parents find they have little or nothing
> in common . . . the empty nest syndrome.

> The outlook for empty nesters can be quite good. They
> can work it out. . . . if you allow your negative feeling
> about the past to take charge of your future, then you're
> cheating yourself. . . . something can be drawn from the
> balance of time couples spend with each other and
> apart. If they're comfortable with each other and with
> other people, then I think that's a sign of a good
> relationship.[2]

When the children move out, warm love and companionship need to intensify. Having a partner cushions
the shock of the vacancy, as early in marriage it cushions the disappointments that occur in young adult
lives.

The seventies have been clouded by a financial
monster called inflation. When in the space of one year
the buying power of money decreases at least ten
percent, the media flashes the alarm: double-digit
inflation! Similarly, in the emotional climate of many
homes, parents of grown children find themselves
face-to-face with a shrinking personal portfolio—children whose lifestyles will not stretch far enough to buy
old-fashioned virtues. The Bible describes many such
baffled parents—and has very few words of comfort for
them.

One case in point is Samson. What brighter beam
could have shone into the home of Manoah and his wife
than the angel of the Lord, who appeared one day to
that cheerless, despairing couple?

"You are sterile and childless, but you are going to conceive and have a son," he said. Too good to be true, they thought! But it was exhilarating, and it *was* true!

"See to it that you drink no wine or other fermented drink . . . no razor may be used on his head. . . ." The Nazirite vow! In the decadence of Israel this boy would stand out. He would conform to the stringent code set out by Moses (Num. 6:1–21) for that special few who dedicated themselves wholly to the Lord and led strict lives of devotion and consecration. Undoubtedly, Manoah gratefully accepted his assignment.

With utmost care Manoah and his wife double-checked the announcement (Judges 13). Were there ever two parents more willing to obey and more expectant of God's blessing? "The woman gave birth to a son and named him Samson; and the child grew up and the LORD blessed him. And the Spirit of the LORD began to stir him . . ." (Judg. 13:24,25).

Samson, as far as the biblical records show, grew up in his home territory with proper training, devout parents, and God's blessing. But the next chapter crashes upon us with a deafening explosion: "I have seen a Philistine woman in Timnah; now get her for me as my wife."

Samson's request defied everything he had been taught. No decision could have insulted or struck harder at his parents. He was rejecting his home, his people, and the expressed command of God not to intermarry with idolatrous nations. Moreover, the Philistines were a chronic military headache to Israel. By any standard, Samson's request was contrary to all Manoah had hoped and planned for his special miracle child.

Had Manoah, in his fervent desire to train Samson,

overprotected the boy? Had Samson been sheltered too much, not given an adequate basis for judging right from wrong? The Scriptures are silent on the subject; only the devastating sequel speaks. Samson was permitted by God to "blow apart" all that his parents built into him. Not only did he marry outside the faith, but he used his unusual gift of physical strength and his love of fun and life to play games with the lives of others. He lived a reckless, undisciplined life, reeling from one crisis to the next, spiraling from the top to the bottom, from the leadership of Israel to the ignominy of prison with his eyes gouged out.

The scene of his catastrophic death, Samson's destruction of the temple in a final burst of vindictive energy, provokes a scene of family mourning. "Then his brothers and all his father's household came down, took him, brought him up, and buried him . . . in the tomb of Manoah his father" (Judg. 16:31). Without question, Manoah went to that same grave years earlier with a broken heart. It is safe to say he never understood why his life had turned out the way it had.

Although centuries of "progress" have intervened, families continue to grieve over children who go astray. They have many blessings but repudiate them and seem not to care that they break the hearts of those who love them most. Man has many answers — usually he blames the already-bruised parent. Like Job's friend Bildad, he comforts with an accusing finger.

> "If your sons sinned against Him, then He delivered them into the power of their transgression. . . . If you are pure and upright, surely now He would rouse Himself for you and restore your righteous estate. . . . If you return to the Almighty, you will be restored; if you

remove unrighteousness far from your tent" (Job 8:4,6; 22:23).

The result of such reasoning is guilt. Possibly no one staggers under a heavier load than the parent who blames himself for his child's defection.

Double Bubble of Buoyancy

Parents, in almost all cases, influence children the most. Blame for failure of sons and daughters, then, routinely boomerangs on them. Do we rightly brand as losers those parents whose children "wipe out"? Did not the biblical priest Eli lose his leadership because he was a poor father? It is true; Eli forfeited his right to ministry. God said:

> "Why do you kick at My sacrifice and at My offering which I have commanded in My dwelling, and honor your sons above Me, by making yourselves fat with the choicest of every offering of My people Israel? . . . those who honor Me I will honor, and those who despise Me will be lightly esteemed" (1 Sam. 2:29,30).

But let us not stomp parents into the ground with harsh abstractions. The accusation against Eli centered on greed and misplaced priorities. He taught his boys to make a physical profit out of a holy ministry. The parent who is guilty of inverting his values, of placing his children—or anything else—before his worship of the God who made them deserves God's wrath and punishment.

But what about godly, trusting, praying parents? What does God say to the Manoahs and their wives? What comforts brokenhearted, disappointed parents who thought somehow God would turn it all around, and He didn't? They can hold up their heads on at least two counts. There are two flotation rafts, as it were, to hold up these exhausted and sinking parents.

With the perspective of the middle years comes the realization of an important parenting principle: No one person holds all the keys to any one life, not even mothers or fathers. We need to put the yoke of responsibility where God puts it — on the shoulders of the individual. We shall all stand before the judgment seat of Christ: "Each one of us shall give account of himself to God" (Rom. 14:12). If God requires that we stand on our own two feet before Him, then I and my children are each answerable for our own decisions.

The second word of encouragement to parents radiates from the theme of God's eternity. "I, the LORD, do not change" (Mal. 3:6). "I will never desert you, nor will I ever forsake you" (Heb. 13:5). God takes a long-range view, and therein lies our parental uplift. The oft-quoted verse, "God causes all things to work together for good to those who love God . . ." cushions the Christian mother. The final product is not determined by one isolated turn of events or a single decision; it is made from all of them together. Like the ingredients of the batter in the mixing bowl, it takes the complete blending — and baking — of all together to bring out the final product. And the ultimate is glimpsed at the end of our Father's Word:

> "The tabernacle of God is among men, and He shall dwell among them, and they shall be His people, and God Himself shall be among them, and He shall wipe away every tear from their eyes; and there shall no longer be any death; there shall no longer be any mourning, or crying, or pain; the first things have passed away" (Rev. 21:3,4).

The Lord tells parents to keep their eyes on Him. He *will* put all the pieces back together. He *will* remove the hurt. But his finished product may not be evident in our lifetimes.

Voting the No-Children Ticket

Many middle-aged parents are aghast at the "alternatives" of today's young people. Don't have kids, they say. It costs too much — in money, in time, in loss of personal freedom — and "just look at the grief people have with them."

Refusing to have children is like turning one's back on the throne. We do have the right to abdicate our opportunity to bring children into the world, but with that decision goes the ultimately greater grief of never knowing the joy of giving to the world a unique life. Anne Morrow Lindbergh, mother of six, said that what a woman resents is not so much giving herself in pieces as giving herself purposelessly.[3]

Divine wisdom reminds us, "Children are a gift from the LORD; the fruit of the womb is a reward. . . . Blessed is the man whose quiver is full of them" (Ps. 127:3,5).

Technology has given us the privilege of choice, but with choice goes sobering responsibility. When God has built into us the equipment with which to reproduce our kind, dare we make use of it exclusively for our own passing pleasure?

I have a friend who, while studying at an eastern university, became a passionate "women's libber" and a self-proclaimed childless career woman. Then Larry fell in love with her, and under the warmth of his love I saw her thaw out like a T-bone steak in the Texas sunshine. In time, a daughter was born to them, then a son, and recently I received an announcement that twins also have put in an appearance. Her note said: "We now have four kids under four. God really has an all-knowing sense of humor to do this to *me*—I used to think I was non-domestic and had no time for kids. . . . He is teaching me how to cope calmly and even joyfully. . . ."

The rewards of motherhood are sometimes subsurface; one has to dive in to discover them.

Offspring Outward Bound

The exodus period in our family spanned at least ten years. With four children plus assorted in-and-out friends, togetherness at times provoked restlessness.

"I'll sure be glad to get out of *here*," our oldest snorted during her heady senior season of high school. Then it came—that day when we shipped the trunk, when her room became a silent museum, and when phone and mail services were appreciated more than ever.

"Daddy?" she called unexpectedly. "I know I'm not supposed to come home until Christmas, but there's a bunch of kids who are driving to Dallas for Thanksgiving, and I was wondering . . ."

We stretched the budget a little tighter and rearranged schedules—of course we wanted to see her, if only for a weekend.

Then one day came a new (and outlandish) boyfriend, invasion of conflicting standards of behavior, academic skids, and eleventh-hour recoveries.

Coming up on the inside track was child number two, ready to leave with his radically different set of plans and expectations. He would have to try his own wings in occasionally unorthodox, un-family ways. He would be the first to announce that due to "previous arrangements" he could not make it home for Christmas.

On his heels the third child was knocking at the door to adulthood.

A huge contingency of American mothers know the lifestyle well — a blur of carpools; "care packages" to starving students; calls at midnight; arguments over airline reservations "which *could* have been made thirty days in advance!"; mental notes that we are certainly not going this way again with the younger one — a steaming hash of underdone/overdone activity and tension, served with sweet and sour sauce.

Then, in the onrush of the frantic pace, the first alarm rings: "Mother, I have something very important to tell you!" Her voice is dressed in light, airy eloquence. "He asked me to *marry* him."

Your answer aims for frivolity: "Well, I'm glad they're still doing that these days." Inside you turn momentarily white. You add another lane to your personal freeway — wedding preparations.

You've lived long enough to know this is once-in-a-lifetime for all of you; it's worth every expenditure of your maternal capabilities—planning, shopping, phoning, laughing, arguing, praying, putting on the party face, commiserating at midnight with a grumpy husband, consoling the bride-to-be in the nighttime asylum of the backyard where she has fled to shed tears of frustration with the dog. . .

"Yes, Mother, it was a nice wedding, and we're so glad you could come and be with us," you reflect to a grandma gone home. "We'll send you the pictures when we get them." You add up the costs at tax time and wonder how it all happened so fast. You write another letter, and you miss her — oh, so much more than you ever thought you would.

Mainstream Americans have removed most of the reduced speed zones; our lives cruise at the maximum human miles per hour. Mothers caught in the teen traffic know that somewhere out there there's an exit ramp, but we never expect to reach it as soon as we do. We learn to live with the lights and sirens and speeding emergencies, dreaming of the quiet days ahead and, yes, idealizing how nice it will be to relax and watch our children building their adult inglenooks.

Now it seems that suddenly we're there. The father of the bride is using a frayed towel, his shoes need new soles, he could use a new suit, and he wants a new wife. Oh, not *another* wife, but. . . .

"Sweetheart, remember how we used to walk in the woods, just the two of us? Why can't we. . . ."

You readjust the focus on your private thoughts. Feelings and concerns sink into the sublayers of your heart. The seasons seem shorter and, oh God, if it weren't for You . . .

The children are gone. Well, not really; they will always be a part of you. Wedding pictures fill the albums, and you are learning to cherish by remote control. Your heart wants to give too much, go too often; your head holds you back to allow them breathing and growing space. A new prayer shoot emerges in your life — you tell the Lord all about it. ". . . in everything, by prayer and supplication with thanksgiving let your requests be made known to God" (Phil. 4:6).

Rearranging the Empty Nest

Why is it that newlyweds together in a house can be blissfully happy, while twenty-four years later the same couple in the same house are lonely, bored, and soured with each other? Do homes, like cities, have to wither and die when traffic detours around them? Is there a kind of domestic destiny that decrees that the post-childrearing years are barren?

Of those first shocking hours alone the inimitable Erma Bombeck writes, tongue-in-cheek:

> As I walked into my son's empty room, I felt I was in the presence of a shrine. Everything was intact, just as he left it. I fondled the sherbert glass with the petrified pudding under his bed . . . ran my fingers lovingly over his drum that leaked oil on the carpet . . . and cried softly as I tiptoed around the mounds of dirty underwear that didn't fit him anymore. . . . I noticed he had an entire wall with nothing on it, so I moved the pump organ from the hallway into his room. I also discovered by moving out his drums and storing them I could put my sewing machine in the corner with a table. . . . As we were making the change, my husband observed there was an entire closet free. . . . By discarding five years of SPORTS ILLUSTRATED my son had saved, we found room for the Christmas decorations and the carton of canceled checks.[4]

All stories do not have happy endings. There is a growing number of would-be grandmothers who are watching the curtain come down on the family finale. No spark of desire for an encore is burning. Their children simply do not want kids, and they are not having children — period! There will be no sequel in their self-directed drama.

"Oh, Mom! This is a cruddy world. And we've got

too many screaming delinquent brats around anyway! Somebody's got to cut down; besides, we're not cut out to be mom and pop—like you!"

The list of alibis lengthens—money, pollution (moral and physical), overpopulation, personal fulfillment, societal uncertainty. Like a line of clothes in the breeze, our young adults string out excuses for not having children. Some couples have valid health reasons; many reach into the large pool of unwanted babies and encircle them with personal love and care. Still other young couples bend every effort toward a ministry where they make possible spiritual birth in developing lives, spending themselves sacrificially. Hidden away, however, are mothers who know they will never be grandmothers in any sense, and the cold reality chills them to their innermost beings.

Childlessness carries a peculiar pain throughout the Bible. It is used by Isaiah in poetic reference to Judah's captivity. God understands that kind of hurt, and His promises for healing are eternal. As He spoke to His suffering people, He also tells us to lift our eyes and look beyond this life.

> "Shout for joy, O barren one, you who have borne no child. . . . Fear not, for you will not be put to shame; neither feel humiliated, for you will not be disgraced. . . . My lovingkindness will not be removed from you, and My covenant of peace will not be shaken," says the LORD who has compassion on you (Isa. 54:1,4,10).

What about today? A practical suggestion: There are still many young people who highly esteem second-generation contacts. Foster grandparent programs provide mutual enrichment for both young and old. Why not offer babysitting service or consider working at (or managing) a child-care center? Loneliness is almost always by choice; people cluster in churches, clubs, groups of all kinds. We can get involved if we want to, if we look patiently for a place and ask God to lead. He knows where there are children who need us.

Although children leave an indelible print on our hearts, mid-life says "move on." The curtain is rising on the next act.

4
Fair Market Value of Freedom

Her world was falling apart—not her personal sphere of living, but her community, her country was crumbling against the ruthless bombardment of greedy neighbor nations. The roads were unsafe for citizens to travel; life in the villages was chaotic and strained with fear. And even worse, no one seemed to care. Men of the military were apathetic; nobody wanted to defend their ragged borders, much less launch an offensive. Deborah was deeply concerned.

The Israelites, supernaturally sprung from the Egyptian trap, had with great effort traversed the wilderness under the able leadership of Moses. They had fought their way, town by heathen town, into the Promised Land under General Joshua. With God's help the victories had been decisive and could have been lasting. The aged, battle-scarred Joshua warned his young countrymen:

> "The LORD has driven out great and strong nations from before you; and as for you, no man has stood before you to this day. One of your men puts to flight a thousand, for the LORD your God is He who fights for you, just as He promised you. So take diligent heed to yourselves to love the LORD your God. For if you ever go back and cling to the rest of these nations . . . and intermarry with them . . . they shall be a snare and a trap to you, and a

whip on your sides and thorns in your eyes, until you perish from off this good land . . ." (Josh. 23:9–13).

For a short while Joshua's men fought successfully, but soon economic advantage took priority over military security. Why kill off everybody in a vanquished city when a good labor force could be salvaged? Thus it became their practice to move in, take charge, and subjugate the people (letting them keep their places of worship). In time a new generation grew up "who did not know the LORD, nor yet the work which He had done for Israel" (Judg. 2:10). A series of judges ruled, and with each judge a cycle of repentance for wrongdoing was followed by restoration. Then the people would sink more deeply into disobedience against God's commands.

Restless Woman

Deborah saw people suffering under the cruel oppression of the Canaanite king, Jabin, whose commander Sisera commanded nine hundred iron chariots. It seems no man had the courage to defy him. Deborah defined herself as "a mother in Israel" (Judg. 5:7) — a concerned mother, the energetic wife of Lappidoth.

She was a woman of wisdom and insight, a prophetess, and her leadership was recognized by the people as she held court under a palm tree. As she handed down her decisions, did she note with dismay that haggard shuffle of defeat and hopelessness in her people? Or did she sense a latent spark of hope "if only we could get organized"? Something lit in her a torch of retaliation against this overbearing oppressor. She seems to have inquired of the Lord about it, since she readied her plan with speed and precision.

"The LORD, the God of Israel, has commanded," she ordered Barak, a man from the tribe of Naphtali, "Go and march to Mount Tabor, and take with you ten thousand men from the sons of Naphtali and from the sons of Zebulun. And I will draw out to you Sisera, the commander of Jabin's army, with his chariots and his many troops to the river Kishon; and I will give him into your hand" (Judg. 4:6,7).

Apparently suspicious of the authenticity of such a preposterous idea, Barak bargained: "If you will go with me, then I will go; but if you will not go with me, I will not go" (v.8).

The sleeping giant, Sisera, roused himself and his chariots and headed for the Kishon River. Marching toward him, Deborah continued to encourage Barak: "Arise! For this is the day in which the LORD has given Sisera into your hands; behold, the LORD has gone out before you" (v.14). Like a determined mother, she pushed her little boy onto the stage to perform.

The battle turned into total disaster for Sisera. He was overcome by an inundating cloudburst that stalled the chariots in the mud and made his men easy targets for the Israelites. Sisera deserted his troops and fled on foot to the tent of a woman named Jael. When he pleaded with her for water she invited him in, gave him warm milk, and when he fell asleep drove a tent peg through his head.

If this were just an ancient tale it would have little relevance for twentieth-century America, but behind the scene of obsolete battle tactics shines a woman. She is the reason God included the story in the Bible. She was, in her generation, a woman of influence in a world of indifference.

Woman of Influence

The Christian woman in modern America is indebted to this early-day "career woman" for clearly modeling several principles for functioning outside the home.

(1) *Community concern leads to solutions.* There is a bookstore in a bustling residential suburb of Dallas because a friend of mine wanted people to have Christian reading material. She and her husband watched the new subdivisions crawl away from the inner city; they realized there was no Christian literary distribution point within miles of many homes.

Almost as an experiment, they rented a small space across the street from the new post office. Her husband kept the accounts and offered advice; she ran the store with the part-time help of her teen-age daughter. The store now pays tuition for that girl's education, as well as providing a vital service to the community.

Any woman who sets out to participate in community affairs, whether through a job for pay or through volunteer effort, must know why she is participating or her work is wasted effort.

(2) *Use your gifts.* The New Testament clearly teaches that every person who makes a personal commitment of faith in Christ is indwelt by the Holy Spirit and is given gifts or abilities with which to function in the family of God. This is not a talent; talents are innate skills developed by training. Talents are techniques and methods that may instruct or inspire on the natural level. Spiritual gifts are given to build up and strengthen the members of the body of Christ. ("To each one is given the manifestation of the Spirit for the common good" 1 Cor. 12:7.)

Armed with natural competence and the supernatural gifts God gives, a woman can plot her course toward fulfillment in life. Deborah apparently possessed keen judgment and was an expert decision maker. Her ability led her into her life work with success and satisfaction. Many women, especially postgraduate housewives, ask: "What can I do?" (meaning, "How can I earn a living?").

The answer calls for close evaluation. Have I always worked with my hands — needlework, flower arranging, gift-wrapping? Or am I a natural with numbers — balancing the checkbook, helping the kids with math and science, figuring grocery prices in my head? What about linguistics — do words fascinate me, do foreign languages come easily, is spelling a breeze? For many middle-aged women who want to enter the work force or a new ministry, the expenditure of fifty dollars or so to take an aptitude test is worth the investment.

(3) *Keep priorities straight.* Although we may know why we are pursuing our goals, and although they may be in line with our capabilities, it is crucial that we not violate convictions or fail to work according to proper priorities. For example, a Christian woman who serves as secretary to a man who produces pornographic films corrupts her conscience. How do you avoid this dilemma? Know what your priorities are before you start. Here is a practical list for prudent women:

My body. Since this physical house in which I live belongs to Christ, it must be treated with respect. ("Do you not know that your body is a temple of the Holy Spirit who is in you . . . you are not your own? You have been bought with a price: therefore glorify God in your body" 1 Cor. 6:19,20.) This fact forms a basis for my moral code, my belief about abortion, my personal balance of food intake, sleep, exercise, and amount of stress.

My home and family. Throughout the Bible God places importance and honor upon those He has given by blood relationship. ("Honor your father and mother" Eph. 6:2. "If anyone does not provide for his own, and especially for those of his household, he has denied the faith, and is worse than an unbeliever" 1 Tim. 5:8.) My efforts must constantly bring families together, not tear them apart. Our Lord healed Peter's mother-in-law, restored a dead son to a widow at Nain, and reunited Lazarus with his sisters.

Real issues. Many women are lured into occupations, paid or volunteer, that are glorified wheel-spinning. A current banner being waved is "equality for women." This is not a real issue. Women are already equal. They were declared so by God (Gal. 3:28) as well as by our government in our constitutional amendments. We need to ask whether or not this effort is a valid struggle. To get more women into board rooms or executive offices regardless of aptitude or qualification is fraud.

Another subtle trap is to work solely "to make some money." Our Lord warned against the deceitfulness of riches (Matt. 13:22). He clearly stated, "You cannot serve both God and mammon [money]" (Matt. 6:24). To take a job because you think money is the most important thing is to lie to yourself.

Authority of God. Whatever the circumstances of daily life, unless we concede that God rules, our lives will be futile. The Creator who orders the sunrise and coordinates the seasons, who clothes the lily of the field and watches the sparrows, has full right to tell me what to do. And He has promised that He will: "I will instruct you and teach you in the way which you should go; I will counsel you with My eye upon you" (Ps. 32:8).

Making Waves

Christian women are asking questions about assertiveness. A brochure I have lists the following topics to be taught in a management seminar: "Saying what you really mean," "Getting your good ideas across," "Handling conflict," "Saying no." Why do women feel such characteristics are somehow unchristian? These concepts have been in the Bible all along. Paul spoke of "speaking the truth in love" (Eph. 4:15). Isn't this saying what you really mean?

Paul certainly was effective in getting his message across. He knew what he wanted to say: "I determined to know nothing among you except Jesus Christ, and Him crucified. . . . My message and my preaching were . . . in demonstration of the Spirit and of power, that your faith should not rest on the wisdom of men, but on the power of God" (1 Cor. 2:2,4,5).

In regard to handling conflict, the Bible says: "If a man is caught in any trespass, you who are spiritual, restore such a one in a spirit of gentleness . . ." (Gal. 6:1).

On saying no: "Let your yes be yes, and your no, no; so that you may not fall under judgment" (James 5:12).

Stiff Spine for the Business World

From the beginning, God intended women to be "workers at home," as Paul wrote to Titus (2:5), and the home remains a top priority. But the reality of the present day gives no choice to some women. Deborah, of God's ancient people, was faced with a "do-or-die" decision. She crossed over the boundaries of the divine intention for women only when her nation faced disaster. Twentieth-century women cannot appreciate what courage was required, what censure she invited as she violated social mores to achieve her country's victory.

Christians must understand that any decision to tear down the family plays into the hands of the enemy. Atheist Madalyn Murray O'Hair has said, "We must do away with the concept of sex as the modifying differential. . . . Families are our biggest problem."[1]

When a woman knows she is led of God to step out of her traditional role, as did Queen Esther of Persia and Lydia, the businesswoman in Acts, she may proceed with confidence. Nevertheless, operating from a commercial rather than a domestic base means going to battle in a personal sense. Any businesswoman can testify to the killer instinct of the economic arena. Competition is its code name. The Christian woman who works in the world of trade and commerce needs a gritty and vigorous faith to sustain momentum.

Carrie, a schoolteacher, was constantly irritated by her fourth-grade class. Discipline was a problem and, worse, the other teachers ridiculed her honesty and high standards. Carrie related the situation to our group as a prayer request.

"Do you think God wants you in that job?" someone asked.

"Oh yes. There's no doubt that He opened up the job for me."

"Well, then, let's thank Him for that," the prayer leader said. "If He gave it to you, He'll show you how to manage it." She was telling Carrie what Paul told the

Philippians: "It is God who is at work in you, both to will and to work for His good pleasure. Do all things without grumbling or disputing" (Phil. 2:13,14).

God's standards for work quality are very high because we use His name and His power. "Whatever you do, whether in word or deed, do all in the name of the Lord Jesus, giving thanks through Him to God the Father" (Col. 3:17).

Jenny was widowed suddenly, left with two teen-age daughters to support. She was a devout Christian mother with no work experience. She enrolled in a business school and eventually became secretary to a Christian business executive. Now, years later, with both daughters married, she still functions as an efficient "front person" for the same busy executive. She has served with distinction in a key slot.

Not all working women can relate glowing stories of success. Bettina had to start working when her husband died of cancer. She took a government job, although she disliked the hours, many of the people, and found the work boring. Yet she felt she was too old to start new training, and since seniority counted she hung on. She developed health problems and has been a genuine concern to her family. Retirement will be welcomed.

The ideal working situation eludes many women. They would love to stop working or change jobs, but they cannot. Esther has worked for many years and is within two years of retirement. New rules now require her to lift heavy loads, which cause severe strain on her joints and consequent pain. Her requests for transfer to new responsibilities have been ignored. She is trying to "hang on." God's grace *is* sufficient (2 Cor. 12:9) and He alone can carry us through when human weakness threatens to overwhelm us.

Being the Boss Lady

On rare occasions God moves women into leading roles, as He did with the biblical Queen Esther. A survey of CEO's (chief executive officers) reveals the kind of pilot light that burns inside this brand of person.

It starts with what I call a fire in the belly . . . setting "unattainable" goals and then achieving them.

I'm a captivated captive who loves it. After all, it's what I wanted most since I was a kid.

I was aided along the line by my willingness to work long hours and get my hands dirty, by technical competence, and a readiness to make decisions and assume responsibility. Many say they want responsibility but not too many step up and say, "I'll make that happen," and then do.

Important attributes . . . for corporate captaincy are: imagination, creativity, hard work, and probably the most important of all—judgment.[2]

Is there an enigma here? A contradiction? How can God tell women to be "workers at home," as Paul says to Titus, and at the same time allow women in—even appoint them to — positions of leadership and high visibility? What does this do to the principle of submission?

Evangelical leaders disagree. Bible scholars refute each other's interpretations. And women continue to take control, with or without the approval of male

Christian leadership. It is my conviction that we are essentially asking the same question asked of Christ about divorce: How can You reconcile legal divorce when God's law already states, "let not man put asunder"? Jesus' reply was, "Because of the hardness of your hearts" it was permitted (see Matt. 19:3–9).

Our world has strayed far from God's intention that a woman should be a contented and creative family member, moving out into the community in various ways but always safely within the shelter of a loving circle of home folks. Instead we have fragmented families and isolated single parents; we have fueled our women with questionable goals.

Women have an enormous store of energy and potential to serve. Many female minds are excitingly creative and are cradled in temperaments that reach for challenges. These women will be, almost in spite of themselves, leaders. Of this breed of person one author writes:

> Some people may have greatness thrust upon them. Very few have excellence thrust upon them. They achieve it. They do not achieve it unwittingly by "doing what comes naturally"; and they don't stumble into it in the course of amusing themselves. All excellence involves discipline and tenacity of purpose.[3]

When women who are natural leaders combine that leadership with a vital relationship to Jesus Christ, the results are incredibly attractive and beneficial.

Our rapidly spinning offspring of Adam and Eve desperately need input from women who have "got it together" with God and man. Who is better equipped than a woman who has lived long enough to get the feel of life and knows where she herself is going? *Business Week* said (November 4, 1975): "... we can no longer afford to under-utilize the talents of half of the [American] population." The doors are open for women to make a difference, but it is a world of danger and subtle distortion. We women enter at our own risk, and we have no right to be there unless God says "go."

Choosing the Low Profile

Freedom to choose also includes the right *not* to become involved in the grinding gears of the workaday world. A middle-aged wife most often finds the crafty competition of commerce a stiff current to row against. Moreover, her husband is also facing a strong headwind and needs her backup support at home more than ever before. At today's torrid pace it takes two to survive, especially if the man shoulders heavy executive responsibility. Wise is the woman who keeps herself whole, healthy, and helpful — a ready and willing wife and lover—to enjoy unencumbered years with her spouse, to laugh and play and piece together available hours with family and friends, making a priceless patchwork of memorable experiences as a legacy to be left and cherished.

The American Christian woman is, without doubt, the most blessed creature of God's creation. We have, in Moses' words, been brought

> "into a good land, a land of brooks of water, of fountains and springs, flowing forth in valleys and hills . . . a land where you shall eat food without scarcity, in which you shall not lack anything. . . . When you have eaten and are satisfied, you shall bless the LORD your God for the

good land which He has given you. . . . lest, when you have eaten and are satisfied, and have built good houses and lived in them . . . and your silver and gold multiply, and all that you have multiplies, then your heart becomes proud, and you forget the LORD your God . . ." (Deut. 8:7–14).

Was there ever a group more indebted to God than we?

5
I'm Expensive, But I'm Worth It

Before I was ready to hear it, my children invariably chirped, "Mommy, I do it myself!" Buttoning a shirt, tying a shoelace, making Granddaddy laugh, cheating on a test, running away, winning a race—a thousand threads are bound together to weave a "self," an increasingly unkempt "me." Someplace along the way the dye sets, and the stains become impossible to erase. As adults, we discover we are pretty much finished products. New ideas are not as attractive as they once were; holes are harder to mend; the notion of "me" clamors for defense against any and all critics.

Toward what far shore does this self-protective wind blow us? Mark Twain (in reality a disenchanted man named Samuel Clemens), prolific author who brought joy to so many readers, wrote:

> A myriad of men are born; they labor and sweat and struggle for bread; they squabble and scold and fight; they scramble for little mean advantages over each other. Age creeps upon them and infirmities follow; shames and humiliations bring down their prides and their vanities. Those they love are taken from them, and the joy of life is turned to the aching grief. The burden of pain, care, and misery grows heavier year by year. At length ambition is dead, pride is dead, vanity is dead; longing for release is in their place. It comes at last—the

only unpoisoned gift earth ever had for them—and they vanish from a world where they were a mistake and a failure and a foolishness; where they left no sign that they have existed—a world that will lament them a day and forget them forever. [1]

Bertrand Russell, the brilliant Nobel prize winner who died in 1970, leaving behind a legacy of more than forty volumes on philosophy, education, politics, and sex, wrote:

We stand on the shore of an ocean, crying to the night and the emptiness; sometimes a voice answers out of the darkness. But it is a voice of one drowning; and in a moment the silence returns. [2]

Similarly, nineteenth-century lawyer and politician Robert Ingersoll stood at the grave of his brother, saying: "Death is a narrow vale between the cold and barren peaks of two eternities. We cry aloud and the only answer is the wailing echo of our cry."

"Myself," it seems, is stuck alone in the mud of melancholy, if these men are to be believed. But the remedy is people, we are told. Caring people make the difference.

Once upon a time there was a frog. But he wasn't really a frog. He was a prince who looked and felt like a frog. A wicked witch had cast a spell on him. But since when do cute chicks kiss frogs? So there he sat—unkissed in frog form. But miracles do happen. One day a beautiful maiden grabbed him up and gave him a big smack. Crash! Boom! Zap! There he was—a handsome prince. And you know the rest. They lived happily ever after. [3]

No, we in the mid-years chuckle and frown at "frogology." We have lived long enough to know that people can help to some extent, but as Bertrand Russell lamented, they are themselves trying to stay afloat. Most people reach out to us while trying to find themselves. What solid, unshifting base can I use to get a look at my own price tag?

Self-Esteem Starts With Reverence of Our Maker

As a young girl, nearly all my clothes were hand sewn by my mother, who was a gifted seamstress. Because I had nothing with which to compare them, I took these dresses, coats, skirts, and blouses quite for granted, until I wore one of those dresses on a date with the man who was to become my husband. It was made of royal blue velvet, and he "flipped" over it. Suddenly I saw my mother in a new light. I began to appreciate her sewing skills. Nobody else had clothes like mine, and I had gained prestige in the eyes of this important person because of my mother.

A blue velvet dress is a weak metaphor for myself, but the example shows how easy it is to take for granted a priceless gift from God and regard our divine Creator as though He were doling out people at piggy-bank prices.

The original idea for me — and you — was literally "out of this world." "Then God said, 'Let Us make man in Our image, according to Our likeness; and let them rule. . . .' And God created man in His own image, in the image of God He created him; male and female He created them" (Gen. 1:26,27). God used Himself as a pattern and He liked His product: "God saw all that He had made, and behold, it was very good . . ." (Gen. 1:31).

The beginning God made for man was the best it could possibly have been. Humans often know something of the excitement of good beginnings. In my own family I saw an infant born to a father who was near-ecstatic over the child, who seemed to have everything a man could ask for in his offspring. His joy and fulfillment overflowed, so that he gave of himself and his means generously.

"Daddy'll let me do it!" became a familiar retort.

The child, who in no way could understand her father's motives, assumed that somehow she was above others, that she was undeserving of reproof and immune to punishment for wrongdoing. Willful and deliberate acts of self-gratification — at the expense of her father's wishes and reputation—increased with the years. The concerned father tried to counter her downward drift with increasing intensity, but in time his health broke, and he died with a grieving heart.

God, like that father, watches our lives flower and fade. An earthly dad can do very little, if anything, to reverse the decline in order to prove his love. Not so with our heavenly Father. He saw the worth of man's perishing life, and He moved to provide escape.

Not only did He make us in His own image, but He also gave His only Son to die for our salvation. "You were not redeemed with perishable things like silver or gold from your futile way of life inherited from your forefathers, but with precious blood, as of a lamb unblemished and spotless, the blood of Christ" (1 Pet. 1:18,19).

Such value placed on our heads raises our ratings in the eternal stock market. If we are made in His image and purchased by the blood of His Son, then what in the world are we doing hiding behind false modesty or lame excuses such as "I'm naturally shy"?

> Shyness is basically a form of social anxiety. It comes from the anticipated fear of rejection . . . the person's reluctance to look you in the eye or to speak up except when spoken to.[4]

Good advice comes from the book *Can You Love Yourself?*

> Now it is your responsibility not to pervert or destroy how God created you, but to enhance and build upon His original perfect creation. If He declared creation good then you must accept the idea that God wants you to believe you are good and develop a good self-image.[5]

Self-Worth Means Self-Working

A common perplexity of parenthood is how to instill in children wholesome self-confidence. I recall struggling with this in frustration with one of my children. Acceptance, clothes, travel, music lessons — nothing seemed to press the button of self-assurance. One day it dawned on me that in one area this child *was* confident —cooking. Why? It was almost too simple to believe.

When I had gone to the hospital for the birth of my younger children, this older daughter had remained at home with Daddy, and he had delegated to her the preparation of meals. She had been virtually on her own—sink or swim, cook or starve.

There was a principle: Performance proves ability, and problems provoke performance. I had made the common mistake of doing too much for my children, not giving them enough tussle with critical targets.

The International Women's Year splashed across the

headlines of our media in 1975. The thunder from feminist generators called loudly for women to assault top positions in business and labor, to get elected to political office, to go into labor unions, and to enter professional sports. Confidence comes from accomplishment, and feminists have rightly assessed that women will believe in themselves when they see what they can do. Many feminist methods may not be biblical, but the basic assumption is sound.

The Proper Source

Confidence can be easily misplaced. Self-identity must be lodged in the proper source, or it is easily jumbled. Written on a restaurant washroom wall were these words: "I have taken the pill, hoisted my hemline above my thighs and dropped it to my ankle. . . . I've rebelled against the university, skied at Aspen, loved two men, married one; earned my keep, kept my identity, and frankly, I'M LOST!" Self-assurance issues from achievement, but only as it builds moral strength.

It is not only the young who lose their way. On Monday, January 22, 1979, the Dallas *Morning News* carried an incredible feature on a male stripper, age twenty-eight, at a local dinner theater show. One sixty-nine-year-old man commented: "I'm shocked and amazed. There are women out there dressed like they'd go to a church banquet, and look at them yelling and screaming at that naked man. I wouldn't even walk around like that around my wife." Almost inconceivably, this young man's deluded mother commented, "It's not dirty; it's fun."

The Real Me: An Inside Measurement

Self-esteem is thinking honestly about yourself. ". . . not to think more highly of himself than he ought to think; but to think so as to have sound judgment" (Rom. 12:3). God wants us to avoid extremes. We should neither rate ourselves too highly, nor should we, as Moses did at the burning bush, plead impotence —an excuse that sparked the Lord's anger.

Jo Berry, in her book *Can You Love Yourself?* tells of a friend who committed suicide.

> She was an excellent housekeeper, had an attractive figure and nice clothes. She was a very capable person but she had an image of herself as being inadequate and useless. She thought about herself in a way that wasn't true. Because of this "thought lie" she became so despondent she took her own life.[6]

When will we learn that the outside woman, no matter how pleasing, cannot make up for bankrupt interiors?

An expert in law asked Jesus Christ what he must do to inherit eternal life. Our Lord summarized the commandments His inquirer knew well: " 'You shall love the LORD your God with all your heart, and with all your soul, and with all your strength, and with all your mind; and your neighbor as yourself' " (Luke 10:26). The implication is that it is impossible to love another person unless we love ourselves.

Self-love is not an emotion; it is a measure of worth, of value. We learn love from God ("We love, because He first loved us" 1 John 4:19). True love, however, is expressed. God showed His love to us by giving us His son; we express a healthy self-love when we use ourselves as God intended. How do I know if I'm doing that? Try the checklist in the "love" chapter—1 Corinthians 13: "Love is patient [with myself?], love is kind [to myself?]. . . . It does not boast [about myself?], it is not proud [of myself?] . . ."

What About When I Just Can't Do It?

One of the most painful experiences of my life was my inability to speak in public. Because I had married an able platform performer, my inability was particularly humiliating. My husband tried very hard to help me, but again and again I "goofed" and became nervous, embarrassed, and totally miserable. Refusing to give up on me, he enrolled me in a public speaking course and insisted that I at least try it. I was terrified at seeing only eight women in a class of forty, but I was relieved to discover that most of the men were more frightened than I was.

Upon completion of the course I had the opportunity to take a second course, tailored especially for women. Then I was invited to take instructor training. This intensified repetition of what I had feared the most pushed me past my self-erected barriers.

Although I had known for years my worth in the sight of God and I truly wanted to overcome my failure, there were emotional bars I could not budge without a big push. The question was: How badly do I really want to change myself?

A Woman Who Used Her Head to Prove Her Worth

Before David became king of Israel, he was forced to play hide-and-seek with King Saul, who was very jealous of him. Hiding out in the desert, David and six hundred men came upon a wealthy sheep-owner whose men were shearing his sheep. Such a band of guerrilla fighters ordinarily would steal from the local herdsmen, but David was friendly and sent a polite message asking for bread and water.

The reply from Nabal was surly and suspicious: "Who is this David? Who is this son of Jesse? Why should I take my bread and water and the meat I have slaughtered for my shearers and give it to men coming from who knows where?"

Angered by this unwarranted rebuff, David set out to do battle.

Meanwhile, one of the servants ran to tell Nabal's wife, Abigail, the state of affairs:

> "David sent messengers from the wilderness to greet our master, and he scorned them. Yet the men were very good to us, and we were not insulted, nor did we miss anything as long as we went about with them, while we were in the fields. They were a wall to us both by night and by day, all the time we were with them tending the sheep. Now therefore, know and consider what you should do, for evil is plotted against our master and against all his household; and he is such a worthless man that no one can speak to him" (1 Sam. 25:14–17).

One can almost see Abigail's shoulders sag. The text describes her as intelligent and beautiful. She had probably attracted Nabal's attention by her beauty, but she would have to save his life—and her own—with her brains. His name, she later told David, meant "fool." He was brash, fast-living, impulsive, and undoubtedly insecure—an early-day macho man!

Abigail not only knew her husband; she knew herself and what she had to do. Quickly she put together meals for David's men and loaded them on donkeys. Riding her own donkey, she met David en route.

"On me alone, my lord, be the blame. And please let your maidservant speak to you, and listen to the words· of your maidservant" (1 Sam. 25:24). She apologized for Nabal's poor manners, reminded David that the Lord had kept him from bloodshed, and begged him to accept her gifts of food.

David immediately recognized her good intentions, her humility, and her faith. He complimented her good judgment and granted her requests.

Abigail is a prototype of many women living with husbands (or others) who act foolishly and endanger those around them. She could easily have underrated herself and her importance to God, but she rose above the moorings of her life. Her personal direction-finder was set on her unchanging God and that put her in the proper position. Had she judged herself by other people, her own compass point might have led her astray. She moved with resolve and wisdom, showing that the race to prevail over difficulties is not to the swift, but to the personally secure.

Packaging God's Product

When a woman truly understands her inside worth, it shows. How does she react in a crisis? Over the long haul, does she hold up or fold up? Are people around her stronger or weaker because of her influence? It all depends upon where her private compass is set.

What else does the world see? In a strange sort of female alchemy, the secretions of self-esteem — either high or low — seep through to the surface in the form of personal body care. The practiced eye of most middle-aged women easily spots a lady of poise. We say she "carries herself well."

How to sit, stand, and walk are the ABCs of most "charm" or "finishing" courses (more recently labeled "successful-woman seminars"). It's part of "body english" to walk with a level head and purposeful stride (with toes pointed straight ahead) instead of a mincing, apologetic step or a rawboned, reckless gait. To sit straight, with legs together and arms relaxed, and to stand with one's spine holding the body in balance, speaks of inner composure.

A woman's voice indicates inward pressure. High-pitched, high-volume, high-speed speech—regardless of the words—means "high-strung."

The choice of clothes in a culture where selection is plentiful is an eloquent clue to our persons. The cut, the color, the cloth—with our particular figures inside—combine to suggest self-portraits.

Controlling all of this physical impression, however, is the face, the mirror of the soul. The eye, our Lord reminded us, is the lamp of the body. What goes through it—in or out—carries long-term effects.

Most women cannot describe their facial shape; (rectangular, triangular, or round) according to bone structure. Nor do they know their skin's undertone, so as to choose the most becoming hair styles and clothing colors. American women have become slaves to current fashion and bargain tags, regardless of personal appearance.

On any day I can open any metropolitan newspaper or magazine and and be bombarded with, "Buy this . . . latest . . . newest . . . sexiest . . ." Sadly, many Christian women have fallen in line, unaware of how subtly they have abdicated their opportunity to make their outward appearances truly beautiful.

Does God care what we wear? He sees every item in our wardrobe. Isaiah lashed the Israelite women mercilessly for their jewelry, the accessories that accented the "festal robes, outer tunics, [and] cloaks" (Isa. 3:16–26). The scathing rebuke came not because of the clothing, but because of the inner pride it conveyed.

Breaking Out of Boxes

Have you ever noticed how life is a series of house arrests? Our earliest confinement is in the body of our mother. We break out of the womb, only to discover that we are restrained by family, home, school, as well as by our own personal guards that produce panic.

I clearly remember a surprise birthday party for my eighth birthday. I walked through the front door of my home to face a roomful of screaming friends. I panicked. My inside sensors blew, and I ran right through the house and almost out the back door before I was stopped. I felt trapped.

Numerous women have confided to me that they feel "boxed in" with their particular sets of circumstances. Either they feel they cannot measure up to the demands on them or they see themselves as too good for the demeaning plights they are in. "I want out!" they are screaming with every action.

Personal freedom is always available to the child of God. No person or thing can bind the soul that sees beyond the box. The tie with the eternal God allows us to elude the knot around our necks, allows me to know who I really am.

6
Blues in the Light

Mickey Mouse, aged and sagging, sat on a park bench talking to a man holding a newspaper bearing the headline: "Mickey Mouse Turns 50."

> Then after Fantasia the big money went to live action. My royalty check stopped coming in . . . Minnie left me. I had to have Pluto put to sleep . . . Huey, Dewey, and Louie became Moonies — but I hear the Duck's doing well—he's a big shot at GAO . . ."[1]

Who, after a half century of teetering on life's seesaw, has not reflected on the past with a wistful backward gaze? Everything in the past is clear, but up ahead clouds shroud the view. Our trip from here on depends on piloting skills; we know we are flying blind. Will we crash? Will it be fatal? What kind of instrumentation do we need in middle-aged weather?

Crash and Burn or Cruise and Ignite?

Pressure and depression go together like a kite and a long tail. Defying a headwind demands steady resolve.

I recently watched a crafty TV reporter query a man suspected of embezzlement. He probed with rapid-fire questions.

"And are you responsible for this account? . . . Did you sign these vouchers? . . . Did you authorize these

payments? . . . Were you not present at the meeting?"
On and on, the skilled investigator drilled holes in the
defense. The interviewee, however, showed no signs
of discomfort—no sweaty brow or fidgety fingers, no
nervous facial giveaways. Instead, he stared straight at
the investigator as he answered. He pitted himself
against the challenger and turned the implicit accusa-
tions into his allies.

It reminded me of a biblical pressure cooker. Elijah,
God's servant in famine-fatigued Israel, received a
rigorous assignment: Go visit King Ahab and Queen
Jezebel and announce impending rain. One rather large
obstacle made the assignment almost fatal. Jezebel, a
devout idolater, was busy killing all the Lord's prophets.

"Is that you, you troubler of Israel?" King Ahab
asked him. Elijah seized the offensive: "I have not made
trouble for Israel, but you and your father's family
have. You have abandoned the Lord's commands . . .
now summon the people." His fearless thrust put the
king on the defensive, and the ensuing confrontation
on Mount Carmel between the courageous prophet and
the prophets of Baal has been retold countless times.

Look at Elijah, however, when it was all over. The
rain came, and in his exhilaration the prophet ran at
least twenty miles down the valley. Then he received an
ominous message from Jezebel—a death threat. Suddenly, "he was afraid and arose and ran for his life and
came to Beersheba [120 miles south!] . . . he sat down
under a juniper tree; and he requested for himself that
he might die" (1 Kings 19:3). Obviously, severe depression was setting in.

Many leaders experience a dramatic "low," especially after the elation of high success. Winston

Churchill called depression his "black dog." Psychologist Nathan S. Kline calls the familiar pictures of Abraham Lincoln "the very portrait of melancholy."[2] But prominent people do not have a corner on depression. The National Institute of Mental Health's 1973 report on depressive disorders said, "During any given year, fifteen percent of the adult population — some twenty million people — may suffer depressive symptoms."

A poignant description of depression appears in *Season in Hell*, by Percy Knauth. The writer claims his "descent into hell" began at age fifty-seven, after he left the security of a large firm where he had worked for more than thirty years.

> I was tired and sad. I felt friendless and alone. I slept badly and was given to long periods of hopeless brooding. I wept often, by myself, in response to the most trivial happenings. I carried an intolerable burden of guilt, much of it associated with things that had nothing to do with me. . . . And most of all, I always felt afraid.[3]

Fighting a Formless Foe

The cure for depression is elusive; the malady overwhelms us when the cause is unknown. We must be careful to distinguish between normal "down" times— such as that caused by the loss of a loved one by death or divorce, deep disappointment, or bodily weariness combined with fear — from true depression. These "blues" have a definable root from which they grow, but true depression, which continues without apparent cause, usually shows itself in a physical slowdown, with fragmented speech, wringing of hands, slumped posture, and a generally dejected appearance. Some people turn to drugs or alcohol or deviant behavior. Compulsive acts or attempted suicide may result. In *Suicide, A Cry for Help*, writer Helen Hosier observes:

> It has been demonstrated that a certain area of the will functions in any suicide and these deep pits of melancholy paralyze to such a degree that the resolution necessary for self-destruction is, in the final analysis, lacking for many.[4]

Suicide cannot be ruled out, however, and this possibility adds to the complexity of the problem.

Two Christian therapists, writing to pastors who counsel depressed persons, warn that depression is often masked.

> It is hidden by symptoms that help the person deny that he is depressed. No one likes to admit that he is depressed. . . . Facial expression can be an important source of clues. Crying spells were frequent. Feelings of hopelessness were usual. . . . suicidal preoccupations were recorded in 32% . . . cramps in the abdomen and pain in the chest or heart region . . . lowering of resistance to pain when they are depressed.[5]

Modern life is mercilessly hard on middle-aged persons. At a time of physical downshifting come peak demands in careers, teen-age troubles, maximum monetary overload, and obligatory care for aging parents. All this happens in a society whose support goes to young people. What does God want us to do with this emotional surcharge? How does He intend for us to use it as ballast instead of a millstone?

As early as 1917, Sigmund Freud analyzed causes of depression ("Mourning and Melancholia"). Mourning, he said, carried a sense of loss, but depression includes a feeling of guilt. Freud theorized that an inner conflict of love and hatred clashes to produce depression. Anger calls for murder, but love rules that out; consequently, hatred is buried and translated into a paralysis of murderous emotion—depression.

Many psychiatrists feel that early childhood pain forms a fertile bed in which adult depression grows. But this does not explain why some persons with traumatic early years never seem to stumble emotionally.

A decade ago, author Lucy Freeman explained human depression in her book *The Cry For Love*. She sees depression as an echo of childhood deprivation of love; hence, her title.[6] Perhaps this has a valid base, but many women have assured me they were definitely loved while growing up, "and I don't know why I'm always so down."

Why Cry?

God's recorded tally of those who shed tears as an outward sign of inward frustrations explains some of the reasons for profound sadness. Jesus Christ Himself wept with Mary at the tomb of Lazarus. The first scriptural record of weeping appears to be when Sarah insisted that Hagar and her son Ishmael leave after the birth of Isaac. Wandering in the wilderness with her water supply depleted, Hagar put her son under a bush and sat down, thinking, "I cannot watch the boy die." And as she sat nearby, she began to sob. David wept over his son. King Hezekiah of Judah wept bitterly in prayer, asking for an extension of his life. Jeremiah wept over the impending exile of the Jews. Judas wept with guilt, Peter in repentance.

The physician Luke records stories of two women who personify the hopelessness and helplessness that fuse into depression (Luke 7). The scene: A widow is the focal mourner in a large funeral procession passing through the gate of the village of Nain. Jesus, at the height of His popularity, is followed by a large crowd of disciples and curiosity seekers. Customarily, such an entourage would step aside and allow the funeral procession to proceed to the place of burial, being careful not to allow even the shadow of the dead body to fall on them, causing ceremonial uncleanness. Instead, Christ "saw her, He felt compassion for her. . . . He . . . touched the coffin. . . . 'Young man, I say to you, arise!'. . . Jesus gave him back to his mother" (Luke 7:13–15).

The widow, whose only companionship and means of support had been removed, had reason to mourn. Realistically, she had nothing to live for. But Christ intervened. What happened? Why? "We do not have a high priest who cannot sympathize with our weaknesses, but one who has been tempted in all things as we are—yet without sin" (Heb. 4:15).

Often, advice to depressed persons is an appeal to reality. "Think—brooding won't help! That's the way life is. Turn energy into positive action. Smile—put on a happy face. Act enthusiastic, and you'll be enthusiastic!" There are kernels of truth in these psychological spurs. But in the fury of the storm, thinking is near impossible. I remember the high fever of my newborn infant son. What if God took him away? I felt fear, panic, anger—very little cool, calm reason. It was not an idea, but a *person* I needed to lift and stabilize me. Physical illness and death shakes us deeply, but much worse is the terror of spiritual disease and death.

Luke follows the deliverance of the widow's son with

what seems to be an extravagant display of penance (Luke 7:36–50).

"There was a woman in the city who was a sinner. . . ." Luke introduces a prostitute in a society where women had virtually no opportunity to be self-supporting. Whatever her reasons, this woman had used her body to earn her bread and in the process had contorted her own spirit and found herself in excruciating emotional and spiritual turmoil.

I once chatted with a prostitute at a women's conference. It was past midnight, and most of the conferees had gone to bed. We sat by a smoldering fireplace as she answered my questions.

"How did you ever get into this life?"

"Needed money . . . wanted love . . . fear of failure in other things. . . ."

"Do you really want to change your living pattern?"

"Yeah, most of the time, but it's the only thing I can do."

"Wouldn't you like to change?"

"I don't think I'll ever change. . . ." I can see her red hair as she stared into the embers, a bundle of tragic and overwhelming conflicts, a young woman stripped of confidence and totally confused. A rational approach to her problems went up the chimney with the smoke. Only an outstretched hand of love could put her in touch with the love that lifts.

So it was with the sinful woman of Luke 7. She came to a Person. Jesus Christ was the only One who cared enough to love without conditions. To come to Him at the home of a Pharisee showed she had inwardly come to the point of no return. With no pride or self-justification left, she was signaling a desperate call for help. Her alabaster jar was probably her life savings, the only thing of value she possessed, saved for burial.

She invited scorn from the leaders with her last-ditch stand. She stood behind Jesus, weeping, broken because of her life of sin. Sorrow, self-hatred, and desperation wiped out any concern about what people thought. She accorded Jesus Christ her worship and to Him she gave her life and her heart. Onlookers saw her as a burned-out shell—what could the Master do with her? True, she was the embodiment of human ashes, but Jesus Christ specializes in resurrection.

How could He, apparently without ceremony, pronounce this wretched woman clean? "Your faith has saved you; go in peace."

His parable, spoken to the host, spills the secret. Two men owed money, He said, and neither of them could pay anything. One owed ten times more than the other, but both debts were totally canceled. Which man, asked Christ, will love the moneylender more? Obviously, answered the Pharisee, the one whose debt was larger. Correct, and this woman whose sins were many has been forgiven—"for she loved much."

The weeping and anointing were outward evidence; the change took place inside. No amount of groveling in the dust because of wrongdoing will erase guilt, but God responds to love and faith in His Son.

7
How to Become a Genuine Antique

Last year I visited my mother and said in a reflective moment, "Mom, I can't believe you are seventy-eight years old. I still think of you as somewhere in your thirties or forties — I guess that's when I was most impressionable. And it's even harder to think that someday I probably will be as old as you are now. Tell me, what does it feel like to be seventy-eight?"

"Well, I hardly know what to say," she replied, "It really doesn't feel any different. . . . I'm still the same person I've always been. Some days are better than others."

"What do you think about when you consider the future?"

At this her eyes dropped, and she shook her head. Finally she looked back at me without words, but her silence and her eyes were eloquent. She did not want to talk about it, but finally she said, "It's all in God's hands."

"Does heaven seem real?" I probed. "Do you get excited about seeing Daddy again?" I knew it was a painful subject, but I heartily dislike bypassing the obvious facts of life. Her eyes filled with tears, and she smiled and nodded yes.

Philosophical Graffiti

What happens between that first breath of the newborn and the last breath of old age? And why does it
happen? What can I do about it? In his personal
reflection on getting older, Gerhard Newbeck observes:

> Getting older is to get further and further away from my
> beginnings. . . . And, getting older is becoming a
> grandfather. . . . In spite of smart insights and sophisti-
> cated second guessing, the truth is that, for me, getting
> older is a burdensome beast. Relentlessly the aging
> proceeds. I can make it more bearable, make the prover-
> bial best of it . . . but I cannot modify it. My existence is
> running out of time. . . ."[1]

This professor from the University of Minnesota is
typical of the humanistic thinker. He sees himself
victimized by the enemy—time.

Ignoring the hole in the donut, a handful of "over-
sixty-fives" were interviewed by a magazine reporter.

> I wrote my first book after I reached that silly milestone,
> and now I have a contract for my third. . . . Anyone
> growing older without enthusiasm has got to manufac-
> ture it. If you don't feel it, *pretend* it. . . . The worst way
> to depart is with "Died for Lack of Enthusiasm," bub-
> bled 82-year-old actress Ruth Gordon.

Veteran statesman Averell Harriman commented:

> Some people are old at 50, while others continue to be
> young at 75 and 80. My secret? I suppose picking
> genetically well-endowed parents helps, also having a
> keen interest in what goes on and having something to
> do. I find the only time I really get tired is when I relax.[2]

What are the stereotypes of youth and age? I
brainstormed characteristics that seem to contrast the

two age groups. Young people seem to be progressive but restricted in breadth; impatient; judgmental; optimistic but naive. In action, their tendency is to be fast-paced and reckless, chasing thrills, and hungry in every sense of the word. Older people, on the other hand, tend to be reflective, thoughtful, cautious, understanding, and broadly realistic. They are slower and more deliberate in their actions; they are sedentary and aware of others.

"Wait! I know *lots* of people who are not . . ." you are saying. Yes, so do I. Undoubtedly, this obsession to classify has led to the old cliche: Age is a state of mind. Satchel Page, famous baseball alumnus, is said to have asked the question: How old would you be if you didn't know how old you are? Every stereotype is contradicted by some striding youth in a seventy-year-old body, or a pitiful abandoned old man at age ten.

Charles Schulz scored again when in his "Peanuts" comic strip he had Lucy ask Schroeder at his keyboard, "I dread getting old — will you love me when I'm old and crabby?"

"You don't have to be crabby, you know," he replied.

"But it's hard to change."

"Not if you change gradually — you could be nice in the morning and crabby in the afternoon."

"But I'd still be old all day!"

No Birthdays for the Soul

Our Creator knew we needed abundant examples of life and death around us in order to understand our own movement through this world. He planted His people in an agricultural setting where animals and vegetation provide audio-visual mini-models of life. We still learn from nature.

Our once-daring dachshund, who was a little black dynamo in his puppyhood, came home one day after being "roughed up" by a much larger dog. At least that was the diagnosis of the vet after treating his wounds. His spirit was noticeably diminished after that encounter, and as he grew older we spotted graying hairs around his mouth and obvious weakening of his vision; he once ran straight into a chain link fence. Eventually he developed "rear end" problems and became a recluse. Like lots of people, he "died of old age."

But he was a dog, and it would be a mistake to draw a parallel between dogs and humans, even though we may see a condensed version of physical life before our eyes. Man is more than a body. The Bible teaches that our bodies decay, but they will be changed and resurrected at a future time. The biblical attention is given to our souls, and it is the care of our souls that seems to affect the aging process most profoundly.

David talks to God about youth in Psalm 119: 9–16, with the question, "How can a young man keep his way pure?" The theme sentence answer: "By living according to your word." Then a series of seven verb phrases explain how God's Word works:

I seek you— an ongoing lifetime goal

I have hidden your word in my heart — defensive weaponry against spiritual foes

With my lips I recount—verbal affirmation of values

I rejoice—a positive optimism

I meditate—purposeful thought life

I delight in your decrees — contentment with godly living

I will not neglect—determination to reinforce objectives

California senator S. I. Hayakawa has said, "What you're going to do after you reach sixty-five was established when you were twenty-two."[3] This is also a biblical thrust.

If satisfaction at seventy depends on the early forecast, then training children becomes incredibly important and deserves our best effort. Our impulse to survive includes a desire for power—first in the family and then elsewhere.

Mothers are familiar with maneuvering in the junior ranks. Our family sometimes had station-wagon scrimmage, in which the singsong script reads something like this:

(From the front seat.) "See, Mommy loves *me* better than you."

"She does not! Cuz I get to sit up there coming home."

"Does too! Cuz I get to read the map for her."

"But I get to carry the present."

"So what's so great about that?"

"It cost a lot of money, and besides, Mommy said I can sit on the aisle and see the bride."

"That's just because you're a *girl*! And who likes girls?"

On and on it would go until I halted the interminable trivia.

Our Lord, caught in the crossfire of His disciples' argument about places of greatness, was hearing an adult version of silly juvenile jockeying.

The seed of greatness, said Jesus Christ, flourishes in the soil of selflessness.

"Whoever receives this child in My name receives Me;
and whoever receives Me receives Him who sent Me; for
he who is least among you, this is the one who is great"
(Luke 9:48).

On another occasion, people were bringing their
babies to have the Lord bless them. When the disciples
became irritated, Jesus said:

"Permit the children to come to Me, and do not hinder
them, for the kingdom of God belongs to such as these.
Truly I say to you, whoever does not receive the
kingdom of God like a child shall not enter it at all"
(Luke 18:16,17).

Learning From Little Ones

What childlike characteristics did Christ prize so
highly? The simple honesty of children was probably
uppermost in His mind. They are what they are,
without pretense; judging from his scathing rebukes of
the hypocritical Pharisees, He desires complete honesty. The children also showed perception, recognizing
that Jesus loved them. What parent has not heard a
toddler ask, "Why doesn't she (or he) like me?" Sen-
sitivity to loving and loathing is keen. No doubt the
expressiveness of children, their willingness to cry, to
laugh, and to interact with people delighted Jesus'
heart. Also important was their childlike self-image,
another aspect of honesty. The kingdom of heaven, he
said, is entered only by those who know how little they
are and how great God is.

Gathering this bouquet of commendable virtues and
projecting it downstream to old age is the core of godly
living. But our world has a way of stripping many
bright young lives of their fresh, eager desires to please
and live for God.

The classic description of the physical ravages of old age is catalogued in the Book of Ecclesiastes. Written from the viewpoint of the upright, hardworking man of the world who has spent his life trying to live prudently, the verses describe in exquisite poetry the infirmities that come (chapter 12):

dimming of the eyes:	"before the sun, the light, the moon, and the stars are darkened, and clouds return after the rain . . . those who look through windows grow dim"
trembling hands and feet:	"the watchmen of the house tremble, and mighty men stoop"
dental problems:	"the grinding ones stand idle because they are few"
ears:	"the doors on the street are shut as the sound of the grinding mill is low"
fears:	"one will arise at the sound of the bird, and all the daughters of song will sing softly. . . . men are afraid of a high place and of terrors on the road"
hair:	"the almond tree blossoms"
ambition:	"the grasshopper drags himself along"

What a contrasting view comes from the aging apostle Paul:

I press on in order that I may lay hold of that for which also I was laid hold of by Christ Jesus. . . . one thing I do: forgetting what lies behind and reaching forward to what lies ahead, I press on toward the goal for the prize of the upward call of God in Christ Jesus. Let us therefore, as many as are perfect, have this attitude (Phil. 3:12–15).

Good News —How Do You Receive It?

It was to a godly priest in Jerusalem that the angel Gabriel was sent after the four hundred silent years since the words of the Old Testament prophets. The time had come to announce the birth of the Redeemer. Devout Jews had looked for the Messiah for centuries; now to Zacharias the promise came: a son would be born to his wife, Elizabeth — miraculously, in their post-childbearing years—and he would be a forerunner to the Savior.

"How shall I know this for certain? For I am an old man, and my wife is advanced in years." Doubt clouded Zacharias's mind, and because he did not believe God's word his ability to speak was taken away temporarily.

Six months later a similar proclamation came from Gabriel to Mary in the town of Nazareth. How differently she received his word! Was it the great age difference? Had the many years of prayer and perplexed longing made the old priest skeptical?

Mary was probably very young, not yet twenty years old. Luke explains that she was greatly troubled and full of wonder. Her response to the news was also a question, but it was a request for amplification, not a question of disbelief. "How can this be, since I am a virgin?" As soon as she understood, she pledged herself: "Behold, the bondslave of the Lord; be it done to me according to your word" (see Luke 1:13–38).

The Christian life is a journey down the same road with everyone else in this somber world. Our bodies grow and deteriorate; outwardly there is little difference between us and non-Christians. But there is a difference. There should be a difference. For the Christian, the light burns on the inside. That which is born of the Spirit, Jesus explained to Nicodemus, comes alive. Paul explained it to the Romans like this:

> For those who are according to the flesh set their minds on the things of the flesh, but those who are according to the Spirit, the things of the Spirit. For the mind set on the flesh is death, but the *mind set on the Spirit is life and peace* (Rom. 8:5,6, italics mine).

In the flesh we age; in the spirit we mature.

> Aging is a negative process. It speaks of wrinkles and trembles, of frosted vision, and spotty hearing. Maturing is a positive experience. It points to greater wisdom and increased patience, to stronger love and enriched understanding. One great purpose of the Christian gospel is to help us grow as persons into a maturity patterned after Christ. Doing the will of God is central to this growth. It is the heart of our relationship with God, a relationship that refines and mellows us, that strengthens and perfects—in spite of the limitations of aging.[4]

Halt: Who Goes There?

At mid-life questions change. We see both the dawn and the sunset. We feel the conflict between production and passivity, between activity and inertia. We climb to the top of the roller coaster, survey the scene from the top, and experience doubts about whether we really want to take the plunge full speed ahead. We look back, we peer ahead, and we survey the people around us.

We ponder the paradox of yielding control and acquiring influence. Both seem to be indispensable. We shed the skin which we hurriedly grew in younger years to impress our world; it no longer fits well. Because we are not really sure of ourselves, we reexamine our inside compartments.

> Here reflections offer a new awareness of ourselves as sexual beings and help create new freedom of expression as well as new tensions between partners. It also brings thoughts of disenchantment and dysfunction. . . .[5]

We develop a sharper sensivity to power structures. We see ourselves in the executive chair; after all, haven't we earned it?

During the discontent of the sixties, the fiction of the "generation gap" spawned a crop of "hippie" jokes. One unsigned poster, depicting two shaggy students, highlights the resentment still harbored toward young people by many middle-aged people:

> I'll run over and pick up my unemployment check and then drop off at the university to see what's holding up my check on the Federal Education Grant check. You go to the free VD Clinic and check on your test; then go to the Free Health Center and pick up my glasses and after that go down and pick up the Food Stamps and slide by the food market and then we'll meet at the Federal Building at 12 for the mass picketing of the Stinking Establishment.

Margaret Mead reminded the world that we have parented the first postwar generation. Rapid change emphasizing self in an overpopulated society, a pervading existential philosophy, absence of suffering, instant gratification—all these things undermine communication. We cannot say to our children: "Yes, I know where you are coming from." The fact is that we do *not*; we grew up in different social soils. Both young and old must learn to trust each other.

Aging demands an eventual reversal of roles. The older ones must at some point hear the bugle call of retreat. Youth must advance. Real progress, however, rolls on the rails of wisdom and understanding. How? The most effective teaching is by example: how to handle responsibility, what to do with the resources of time and money, how to manage physical health, how to increase mental virility, how to appreciate true values—learning from people.

Under the heading, "When Did I Become the Mother and Mother Become the Child?" Erma Bombeck has described how life turns around:

> When will the baby catch up with the mother? When indeed.
> Does it begin one night when you are asleep and your mother is having a restless night and you go into her room and tuck the blanket around her bare arms? Does it appear one afternoon when, in a moment of irritation, you snap, "How can I give you a home permanent if you won't sit still? If you don't care how you look, I do." (Is that an echo?)
> . . . The transition comes slowly, as it began between her and her mother. The changing of power. The transferring of responsibility. The passing down of duty. Suddenly you are spewing out the familiar phrases learned at the knee of your mother: "Of course you're sick. Don't you think I know when you're not feeling well? I'll be over to pick you up and take you to the doctor around eleven. And be ready!"
> "So where's your sweater? You know how cold the stores get with the air conditioning. That's the last thing you need is a cold."

"You look very nice today. Didn't I tell you you'd like that dress? The other one made you look too old. No sense looking old before you have to . . ."

You bathe and pat dry the body that once housed you. You spoon feed the lips that kissed your cuts and bruises and made them well. You comb the hair that used to playfully cascade over you to make you laugh. You arrange the covers over the legs that once carried you high into the air to Banbury Cross.

While riding with your daughter one day, she slams on her brakes and her arm flies out instinctively in front of you between the windshield and your body . . . So soon?[6]

8
Wishing, Wanting, and Winning God's Approval

Living is not a spectator sport. No one, at any price, is privileged to sit in the stands and watch the action from a distance. Being born means being a participant in the arena of life, where opposition is fierce and winning comes only to those who exert every ounce of energy.

Although the Promised Land flowed with milk and honey, it housed strange supermen and bullies. But the Israelites, with God's help, overcame them. "You shall drive out the Canaanites even though they have chariots of iron and though they are strong" (Josh. 17:18).

Caleb was the kind of husband a woman needs — stouthearted and capable. When he was forty, he went on a reconnaissance mission with the "dirty dozen" into Canaan, and gathered an intelligence report that dropped jaws. They brought back food samples and farfetched tales that must have kept them up all night around the fire. All agreed that giants lived there, but only Caleb and his young friend Joshua recommended attacking at once. They were voted down.

Forty-five years later, Caleb was still optimistic: "I am

still as strong today as I was in the day Moses sent me; as my strength was then, so my strength is now, for war and for going out and coming in. Now then, give me this hill country. . ." (Josh. 14:11,12). What was Caleb's turn-on? It was his telescopic vision; he saw beyond the backyard, and it lifted him up and over the fences.

Caught in the Job Logjam

During the Great Depression I remember going next door to run an errand during the dinner hour and noticing that our neighbors were not having dinner. Why not? I asked Mother when I returned home. Well, Mr. W. is out of work now, she said. Later, she "happened" to have some extra ham and potatoes for them, which we had brought home from Granddad's farm.

Recently a columnist related the plight of a man who was fired from his job after working half a lifetime with his company. His wife's letter tells the story:

> My husband had worked for the same company 20 years. I can remember back to the time he started . . . . We were thrilled. It was a real career. He did very well over the years, and we've had a very nice life. . . . He came home from work early one day. He never does that. Sometimes he stays late; I'm used to that. It was a real surprise to see him so early . . . he wanted to talk to me. We sat down at the table in the breakfast room, and before he said anything he started to cry. He was sobbing. He had never cried in front of me before. The first thing I thought was . . . that he had some fatal disease . . . funny what comes into your head . . . . When I got him settled down he told me he had been let go . . . he had no choice in the matter; he was out.

The moment of truth comes over and over again to all

of us, as we learn that our worst dreams have come true.

> What happened was that he completely broke down in the weeks after he was fired. He was virtually immobile. He would just stare at the walls. Finally he said, "I just can't do it. You're going to have to go to work." He had changed overnight. All the years of our marriage he had been a very take-charge man, sure of himself, almost too self-confident. Now he had been fired . . . and it all went away. . . . What was left was a sad, frightened man living in a state of panic.

> I kept telling him . . . to think about it intellectually; he had all the same qualities he had had on the day before he was fired. But he had gone into a daze. It was as if he had secretly believed he didn't have any value all these years. . . . He was devastated. . . . He was like a stranger. . . . After 20 years I saw a side of my husband I never suspected existed, and what I saw was weakness and despair and self-doubt. . . . I don't think I'll ever look at him again and see the same man. . . . I love him just as much, but it's a different relationship now. Being fired did that. It goes far beyond business.[1]

In our precarious world of economics, the rug is easily pulled out from under any of us. A high-placed business executive reported that more than one hundred publicly listed companies lost their independence in 1977 as a result of business takeovers. In a dramatic metaphor, he described the process: "The acquired company has found itself in the position of the male praying mantis, who while it continues copulating with its female partner is devoured from head to rear."[2]

Those men and women—and their families—who slide down the chute in business rearrangements need desperately to know what our Lord taught: "Be on your guard. . . . a man's life does not consist in the abundance of his possessions" (Luke 12:15). Then He told the parable of the rich man, which could be entitled: "Memo to American Merchants."

The rich man was a success, so much so that he ran out of warehouse space. He had so much collateral that he had to reorganize to protect it all. With a smile of satisfaction, he surveyed it and said to himself: "You have plenty of good things laid up for many years. Take life easy: eat, drink, and be merry."

God interrupted him. "You fool! This very night your life will be demanded from you. Then who will get what you have prepared for yourself?"

This is how it will be, warned Christ, with anyone who stores up things for himself but is not rich in the spiritual things of God (see Luke 12:16–21).

Notice that it is not the tally of *things* which God criticized; it is the blank column which listed nothing for eternity.

Teepee Trouble With a Capital "T"

Many stalwart women seem able to bounce back and rebuild after financial storms, but a large number of second- and third-generation women are bleeding internally because of family disorders.

Disappointment in those people in whom we have invested our choicest personal labor and love causes a peculiar decay of the soul. I shall never forget a Saturday morning when I was sixteen. Behind a closed door I heard the sobbing of one whom I loved dearly. I went in to find this woman devastated, even though she had lived through war and deprivation of many kinds. She shared with me her heart, crushed because her daughter had broken her trust, violated her conscience and her virgin purity. Time heals, but scar tissue remains, and only God can part the clouds that hang so low at such a time.

What is the proper response to one who has veered from the path and brought shame and disillusionment to us? Again Paul points the way. A man named Alexander, a metalworker, had done him great harm, Paul said.

> The Lord will repay him. . . . Be on guard against him. . . . At my first defense no one supported me, but all deserted me; may it not be counted against them. But the Lord stood with me, and strengthened me (2 Tim. 4:14–17).

Four strands are woven into Paul's response: (1) Revenge or any defensive retaliation is out of place for the Christian. (2) Learn from the mistakes of others; beware of the pitfalls. (3) Being alone in trouble is scary, but it is not fatal. Our attitude should be one of prayer and understanding for those who desert us in need. (4) The Lord Himself can always be counted on to stand beside us and give us the strength we need.

An airline flight attendant once told my husband that she had gone through an agonizing divorce, but through the experience had found Jesus Christ as her personal Savior. For her it was a refining process — distress distilling pure character. For others, stark terror and anger against God erupts. For them, it's not one big problem; it's a suffocating haystack of thistles.

R-r-ring! Oh no! Not now — in the middle of getting dinner ready. I picked up the phone and cradled it between my chin and my shoulder as I stirred the sauce.

"Yes—oh hi, Ginny!" Her voice sounded unusually harsh.

"I just want you to know I have had it with your God!" (We had been studying the Bible together for some weeks.) "He doesn't love me."

"Now Ginny, calm down. What's the matter?" I turned the burner down and sat down.

"Maybe He loves *you* because you're good or something . . ."

"Ginny, what is wrong? Tell me how you know God doesn't love you."

"Well, it's just everything . . ." I drew from Ginny a long string of grievances — car troubles, friction with her children, money worries. "Why," she asked, "would God let all this happen if He really loves me?"

Ginny had a typical tangled life, full of the consequences of poor decisions.

"If we add six and nine and three together, we're going to get eighteen, right?" I asked her. "Let's say I don't want eighteen; eighteen is just too much for me. What do I do with it?"

That's where she was. Add together the car, the kids, the unpaid bills, and she had an eighteen that wouldn't go away.

"If you can't make eighteen smaller, there's only one way out—you have to get stronger."

The apostle Paul had his own private overload:

There was given me a thorn in the flesh. . . . Concerning this I entreated the Lord three times that it might depart from me. And He has said to me, "My grace is sufficient for you, for power is perfected in weakness". . . . Therefore I am well content with weaknesses, with insults, with distresses, with persecutions, with difficulties, for Christ's sake; for when I am weak, then I am strong (2 Cor. 12:7–10).

Life is thorny, and death has become commonplace. The impulsive lifestyle of Americans is making death almost a casual affair. Our senses have grown calloused from fictionalized accounts of murder splattered across the TV screen and novels. The real thing, occurring en masse on our highways and throughout the homes and hospitals of our land, tends to evoke a superficial response. After two university students in Dallas were killed in a car accident, the comments were casual—the gotta-say-something-but-don't-make-it-too-heavy type:

> We talked about death a lot. She told us we should have a party if she died. If she thought we were sad and crying, then she'd be mad. I mean, she'd tell us to go inside and get drunk!

> We were soul mates. Our philosophy amounts to doing what feels good, you know. What feels good is good for you. It's about like that.

> 'Jack was trying to locate himself in time and space,' said his teacher. 'Then he was going to write it all up . . . and figure out where he wanted to go. . . . But those are all problems he doesn't have to worry about now.'[3]

But they were young kids, we say. Once you live a while you get down to business; you learn by living. Do we? Picture a widow, fifty-nine years old, sitting alone in the pew:

> When all the guilty tears you cried last night have dried out in the light of day, and the hallelujahs fade away into the simple sounds around you. When you realize that the things you thought you ought to feel to make you

real didn't. Don't give up. A great fish doesn't live at the surface for long. Neither does a great God.[4]

It is a great God who makes the difference. And if we cannot call upon Him there is no other. Hear the majestic words of Isaiah:

> "To whom then will you liken Me that I should be his equal?" says the Holy One. . . . Why do you say . . . "My way is hidden from the LORD, and the justice due me escapes the notice of my God"? Do you not know? Have you not heard? The Everlasting God, the Lord, the Creator of the ends of the earth does not become weary or tired. His understanding is inscrutable. He gives strength to the weary, and to him who lacks might He increases power. Though youths grow weary and tired, and vigorous young men stumble badly, yet those who wait for the LORD will gain new strength; they will mount up with wings like eagles, they will run and not get tired, they will walk and not become weary (Isa. 40:25–31).

Freedom in the Foxhole

God never leaves us in the dark for long. A behind-the-scenes dialogue between God and Satan helps to explain how some tragedies happen. Job was a good, successful, God-fearing family man. Of him the Lord Himself said: "There is no one like him on the earth, a blameless and upright man, fearing God and turning away from evil" (Job 1:8). With that kind of stalwart substance to his life, Job could withstand almost anything, it seems. God allowed Satan to afflict Job with the loss of his possessions, his family, and his health.

Some people are bouncy; throw money problems at them, and they manage to recover. Drown them in dashed hopes and losses of all kinds, and they seem to surface. But one last trick in the enemy's arsenal is the hardest of all to overcome. It is ill health. When our bodies, and inevitably our minds, are bombarded with pain and helplessness, a unique stress contorts our spirit. "I loathe my own life," said Job (10:1). When illness stretches into weeks and months — perhaps years—hope is hard to hang onto.

> "If I speak, my pain is not lessened, and if I hold back, what has left me? But now He has exhausted me" (Job 16:6,7).

Listen to Job's description of his physical state:

> "My breath is offensive to my wife, and I am loathsome to my own brothers. Even young children despise me; I rise up and they speak against me. All my associates abhor me, and those I love have turned against me. My bone clings to my skin and my flesh, and I have escaped only by the skin of my teeth" (Job 19:17–20).

Job was fighting the whole world single-handedly from his own personal, stinking trench of affliction.

Lifting the Low Ceiling

Why? Oh God, why? Who of us has not asked that question in our frustration? Before we ask He has already answered. "The testing of your faith develops perseverance. Perseverance must finish its work so that you may be mature and complete, not lacking anything" (James. 1:3,4). Suffering is God's finishing school. Paul, who suffered as much as any Christian, was able to write the rallying call:

> I consider that the sufferings of this present time are not worthy to be compared with the glory that is to be revealed to us. . . . For the creation was subjected to

futility, not of its own will, but because of Him who subjected it, in hope that the creation itself also will be set free from its slavery to corruption into the freedom of the glory of the children of God (Rom. 8:18–21).

"Oh yes, in the sweet by and by—that's always your answer," my great-uncle used to say to my grandmother. "Excuse the language, Aunt Alie, but I am drowning in the _____ here and now!"

C. S. Lewis wrote an infectious essay entitled, "Petitionary Prayer: A Problem Without An Answer." His conclusion, after complaining with eloquence about apparently unanswered prayer, is ". . . we ought perhaps to regard . . . ourselves as spiritual cripples. Yet I do not find this quite a satisfactory solution."[5]

That's just where I am, we say. What's new about that? Lewis reminds us that it was precisely here, in human weakness, where Jesus Christ knelt in Gethsemane. "He chose on that night to plumb the depths of Christian experience, to resemble not the heroes of His army but the very weakest camp followers and unfits. . . ."

Do we really think God is advertising more than He can produce? Ask Abraham. "He did not waver . . . being fully assured that what He had promised, He was also able to perform" (Rom. 4:20,21).

Lord, teach us to pray.

9
The Fine Print
of John 3:16

A bright Sunday afternoon in early fall turned suddenly stormy as we drove into the driveway, parked the car, and came through the back door. The breakfast table was set for one — place mat, glass of water, silverware in order. The television was talking, but where was Mom? And then I saw her—not her, but the body in which she had lived for nearly eight decades, the body that had given me birth. An autopsy confirmed what we suspected: her tired heart had beat its last beat. Very quietly, Mom — so like Mom, with no fanfare—had slipped away to be with her Lord forever.

Limp Upper Lip

After Mother's sudden passing I began to sort out my feelings. Of all human loss, perhaps that of a mother makes the deepest wound. She is the physical link with the past; her departure steals the lid from the lineage and leaves us feeling exposed and unprotected. Flying home after the funeral I wrote these angry words:

Death lurks in the shadows. He erupts whenever possible to satisfy his unending appetite for living human beings. We try to ignore him and hope he won't notice us—or we caricature him and pretend he is really, after all, funny and relatively harmless. Or we become very scholarly and try to face him with a scientific head-on confrontation. We look him in the eye, interview those who've had close encounters, find out what really makes him tick. He just laughs.

Moving as I do from my position of weakness, I must stop, look, and listen to the only credible historical witness to testify personally about the life-death struggle.

As scabs form over emotional wounds, memory replays the past and questions congeal. My vague "Why, Lord?" bows before His Word, already written.

Certain Destiny for Saints and Sinners

What does the Bible teach about death? From one end to the other, the transition from earthly life to the life beyond is clearly marked as a critical intersection. "If there is a natural body, there is also a spiritual body. . . flesh and blood cannot inherit the kingdom of God" (1 Cor. 15:44,50). It would be cruel to tell anybody to just sit tight and try to be good and somehow God will get us all to heaven.

During those critical hours prior to the crucifixion of Christ, the Savior reinforced for His disciples the truths they most needed to know. He said, "I am the way, and the truth and the life; no one comes to the Father, but through Me" (John 14:6). Many will come, Jesus said, who think they should be in His kingdom. "Then I will declare to them plainly, 'I never knew you; depart from Me, you who practice lawlessness' " (Matt. 7:23). The oft-repeated story of the beggar and the rich man who both died clearly describes the impassable gulf between the saved and the lost in eternity (read Luke 16:19–31). But how can that be?

A Chicago television news reporter conducted a series of man-on-the-street interviews in the winter of 1979, asking the question: "Is there life after death?" I watched a burly young man who growled confidently, "No, of course not. When we die, that's it. It's all over. You know, you live, and then you die." Just as the reporter was lowering the mike and the camera was leaving him, the man shifted and added, "I hope!" With that he gave himself away. The question will not dissolve; it must be answered.

Two Jewish men sat talking under a nighttime Judean sky. Nicodemus was an educated Pharisee, as yet not willing to be seen with this rabbi, Jesus of Nazareth. Jesus' words were revolutionary: ". . . that whoever believes in Him [God] should not perish, but have eternal life" (John 3:16). He had already explained that there is physical life (the baby) and spiritual life (a new birth). What you see is *not* what you get—eternally. God sent His Son not to condemn, but to save. A guilty verdict with the sentence of eternal death falls on those who reject Him.

"This is the judgment, that the light is come into the world, and men loved the darkness rather than the light; for their deeds were evil. . . . he who practices the truth comes to the light, that his deeds may be manifested as having been wrought in God" (John 3:19–21).

No place in life are we weaker than in the face of death. No other opportunity comes to show what the light can do as greatly as His resurrection power in life's worst trial.

Curtain Down and Lights Out

Life's tidal waves often come without warning, but
even when the sirens sound beforehand we can never
be fully prepared. "The key to minimizing the impact of
a death in the family, say experts on the subject, is more
honesty on the part of everyone involved."[1]

Facing truth may be good for mental health, but it
cannot blunt the agony. Perhaps this article, and many
others, would be more accurately titled, "Things to Do
at Time of Death." Quiet grieving is outdated; we are
supposed to keep busy and apparently keep talking.

Innumerable people have attempted to say the last
word about death. It is almost amusing that we who are
living think we can explain the dilemma of death. We
talk all around it but we have no answers.

> . . . a growing number of Americans have been look-
> ing for a better way of dealing with the dying. . . . Now
> people are willing to discuss such matters openly and
> candidly. Death has finally come out of the closet.[2]

> Our popular culture treats death impersonally while
> denigrating our human responses to it. . . . TV news
> programs submerge the human meaning of death. . . .
> most of us know more about how to kill another person
> than how to treat the dying or comfort the be-
> reaved. . . . our attitudes toward death are likely to
> come from the mass media rather than from a direct
> confrontation with death.[3]

> She left without even saying goodbye. . . . one moment
> she was here. . . . I blew all my lines . . . the strong
> man, with his violent antipathy toward funerals,
> cemeteries . . . crumpled . . . the mind simply couldn't
> make the transition from a person to a body. . .[4]

> Although it is said humorously that no one gets through
> this life alive, few of us know how to deal realistically

with this inescapable fact. . . . Accepting the death of a loved one does not mean you do not care. . . . you care enough to make the end as pleasant as possible. . . ."[5]

Most people give little thought to the subject of death until they are confronted by the experience in the immediate sense. . . . Because illness and dying have been removed entirely from the home . . . the capacity to deal with and accept these facts of life must be relearned.[6]

Having said all of this and more, we come back to death's inescapable emptiness. There is no way to wash the dregs of death down the disposal.

Nobody Home But Me

Bitter loneliness ranks right beside bereavement in high-decibel distress. The following poem was written by a young husband whose wife had deserted him.

ALONE AND IT'S WINTER

At the moment the valley is dark—I search for light and see the outlines of His love, the shadows reflecting His being, but the radiance of His presence often escapes me.

That He is honing me I am sure—but to fully grasp His purpose and believe that the best is yet to come seems an empty dream, futile and unreal.

I yearn to come home to a house that is a home—full of life and love and laughter. Instead, my house is empty, my bed is cold, my children no longer come home to me—they only visit me—and the clock in the hall is my only companion. It strikes to remind me that a beautiful chapter of life is ended and another has not yet begun.

Yet, I have walked too long with God to know that He gives stones for bread, pain without healing, sorrow without comfort, despair without hope, anxiety without peace — that He takes without giving better in return. Tomorrow will come—and so will He.

I know I am never outside the perimeters of His love because I am his child—and He is my God.*

—Robert deVries

A Half Person

Widows—and, yes, divorcées—carry a certain soot on their spirits. They have known the miracle of two becoming one, and when that one is broken, only a part-person survives. In my book *A Woman for All Seasons*, I described in the chapter on Naomi the plight of my mother after Dad's lingering illness.[7] Because I knew her so well, I can state unreservedly that God alone made the difference in the next twenty-three years she lived. She learned the truth of Isaiah's statement: "For your husband is your Maker" (Isa. 54:5).

Writing about personal sorrow is necessarily detached, because feelings are restricted when they are translated into words in ink. We live through our senses; our fear as well as our relief comes through the avenues of sight, sound, smell, touch, and taste. Our memories relentlessly play back the shock waves of sadness. Even after nearly a quarter of a century, certain songs, certain menus evoke a sudden melancholy and longing for my dad, whose death left such a big hole in my life.

But the loneliness of widowhood in modern life is a peculiar problem. Canadian writer Betty Jane Wylie writes of several stereotypes about widows:

*Used by permission of the author.

There is the biblical widow, poor and sorrowing, with her widow's mite and her struggle to survive. There is the sex-mad, wealthy widow of a simpler society (Shakespeare's plays are full of eager widows), when widows were not such a bad catch. . . . Today, sexual expertise is rampant, widows are a glut on the market, and wealthy ones are rare. . . . Not that a widow is mating. Far from it. Most of the time she's scared, tired, and reticent. . . . All thoughts of marriage aside, even conversation is difficult. Ten, fifteen, twenty years of marriage spoil one for casual conversations. With a new man there are no comfortable assumptions.[8]

As someone said, it's easy to make new friends; it's hard to make old ones.

Hand on My Shoulder

This raises the need for touching. Fondled, hugged, patted, and yes, spanked in our early years, we tend to take for granted being touched by another person. Part of the joy of marriage is the warmth and closeness, the touch of the one who loves you.

Anthropologist Ashley Montague calls skin the oldest and most sensitive of our organs. Cold separation is a harsh reality. Usually, the older we get the less we touch others. Having married a fervently affectionate man, I soon came to recognize that my temperate, frugal heritage in personal relationships contained an unwritten rule: bodily contact, except for handshaking and hello and goodbye kisses, was verboten after the age of six or eight. I embarked upon a personal campaign to color in this blank space with appropriate warm hugs, playful smacks, and nudges. To my amazement, I saw kinships and connections of all kinds blossom and flower.

In fact, my husband and I, convinced of the therapy
of the caress, tried it with Mother when she came to stay
with us. In five weeks we saw a dramatic change. From
a frightened, ailing, tense, and closed-up woman, she
relaxed into a serene poise which allowed her to sleep
instead of sob during the night, to read for the first time
in months, to venture outside for walks, even to laugh
and enjoy mealtimes.

Green Leaves in Winter

What will the future hold? We all speculate, hope,
and feel qualms. I asked Christian women across the
United States what they feared most for the future.
Nearly one in five mentioned aloneness — usually
including the loss of their husbands. Realistically, it is a
good possibility for most of us.

> In 1970 there were over six million widows . . . in the
> United States. By 1985 the number of older unmarried
> females is expected to rise by about three million.[9]

Add to widows the number of divorced or deserted
wives, and the statistic is dramatic. Does the Bible have
anything to say to women who are alone after having
donated their productive years to a man and possibly a
family?

Widows were always a major concern in Hebrew
society. Listen to Jewish leaders:

> Moses: You shall not afflict any widow or orphan (Exod.
> 22:22).

> For the LORD your God is the God of gods and the
> Lord of lords, the great, the mighty. . . . He executes
> justice for the orphan and the widow (Deut. 10:17,18).

Job: The blessing of the one ready to perish came upon me, and I made the widow's heart sing for joy (Job 29:13).

Solomon: The Lord will . . . establish the boundary of the widow (Prov. 15:25).

David: A father of the fatherless and a judge for the widows, is God in His holy habitation (Ps. 68:5).

Jeremiah: Leave your orphans behind, I will keep them alive; and let your widows trust in Me (Jer. 49:11).

God cares about people who are alone. Is it fair to say that too often people who are alone do not care about God? Women, particularly, are conditioned by passive submission. When a husband is removed, there is a strong tendency to blame God for mismanagement and to feel sorry for oneself.

God does *not* make mistakes; He always does what is best for us. Self-pity must be shoved back where it belongs — into the face of Satan, "the accuser of the brethren," who will always say to us: "See, your God doesn't really love you, or He wouldn't hurt you like that!"

Each of us who has a husband should hold a personal daily thanksgiving service for him. If and when our heavenly Father is pleased to remove that human support and companionship, He Himself *will* fill the void. "Even to your old age, I shall be the same, and even to your graying years I shall bear you! I have done it, and I shall carry you; and I shall bear you, and I shall deliver you" (Isa. 46:4). That is the word of our Maker.

But surely there is some kind of widow insurance, spiritually speaking. Obviously, some widows do better than others. During my growing-up years, a childless couple who were close family friends took it on themselves to brighten many days for me with visits to their quaint Pennsylvania Dutch relatives. (One uncle was a candy maker, his acquaintance a unique delight for a little girl.) During the automobile rides and family chitchat, many references were made to "Floyd's bad heart." It seemed to be common knowledge that he was living on borrowed time. Uncle Floyd was an inveterate teaser and jokester, but he was very serious one day in my early teens.

"Jeanne, I will be going to the hospital for some surgery, and I just want to say goodbye." Surgery is not necessarily fatal, and I tried to make light of it, but he kissed me on the forehead and squeezed my hand. After his operation all seemed to be well, but on the third day our phone rang. It was Aunt Grace, and her voice was low and shaky.

"Jeanne, honey, will you tell your mother that Uncle Floyd just died."

"But I thought he was . . ." I spluttered.

"No, honey, his heart just couldn't take it. Just go tell her, and I'll talk to you later."

Upstairs, I cried with my mother. I remember being angry with God and evasive at the funeral. I wanted to run away and somehow wake up from this bad dream. But from Aunt Grace I learned a priceless lesson: preparedness. Before long she had secured a position in the headquarters office of our denomination, where she worked until her recent retirement. She was eternally grateful for the privilege of having lived with Uncle Floyd during the brief years God gave them. She exemplified Jeremiah 17:7,8.

"Blessed is the man who trusts in the LORD and whose trust is the LORD. For he will be like a tree planted by the water, that extends its roots by a stream and will not fear when the heat comes; but its leaves will be green, and it will not be anxious in a year of drought nor cease to yield fruit.

The drought *will* appear; the heat *will* come—that is inevitable. But the deeply rooted believer will stand up tall and function.

Jesus, having risen from the grave, asked Peter (and me), "Do you love me . . . do you truly love me?" Peter answered that he did love the Lord, and Jesus sketched a tiny fragment of his future:

"Truly, truly, I say to you, when you were younger, you used to gird yourself, and walk wherever you wished; but when you grow old, you will stretch out your hands, and someone else will gird you, and bring you where you do not wish to go. . . . Follow Me!" (John 21:18).

The forecast was not sunny skies for Peter, and it may not be for me—or you. Nevertheless, the command is clear: "Follow Me." The implication: "No one can do anything to truly hurt you. You are Mine, and I will take care of you."

One further word — about money. Many older women are hobbled by insufficient income. The shrinking dollar and the skyward cost of living reduce to poverty the state of women who have lived formerly comfortable lives. We who have a policy-making voice in churches and Christian organizations need to articulate the critical urgency for adequate pensions for widows and monetary considerations for older people in general. Privately, we need to monitor older women in our own circle of family and friends. We who see the problem are responsible for remedies.

Reading God's Shorthand

Christians are not exempt from suffering. The Bible reiterates the truth like a woodpecker on the tree: Suffering is part of living. "Man is born for trouble, as sparks fly upward" (Job 5:7). Why, then, does God not remove us when we come to faith? He leaves us here because we are salt and light. "You are the salt of the earth. . . . You are the light of the world" (Matt. 5:13,14).

What does it mean to be salt and light? It may mean what to us is repugnant—being dependent in our old age upon people with whom we don't wish to be.

A friend told me of her father, an intelligent, productive educator, who is going blind. His wife has all she can handle taking care of his parents. What will a blind husband, frustrated because he cannot read, totally dependent on her for his livelihood, do to the dynamics of that home? He's already lived a hard life, having lost his first wife and struggled throughout his career. It seems unfair and totally wrong that he should have to suffer the ignominy of being "an old blind man." It seems too much for his wife.

We hate to admit that we need stretching, trials to force us to give, to think beyond our own needs, to know the fulfillment of ministering to helpless ones.

A recent study on the support system of widows in the metropolitan area of Chicago reveals ugly gaps in our families.

Siblings and relatives other than parents or children rarely appear even in the emotional support systems of the Chicago area. . . . there appears to be an increasing separation in American society of friendships from kin relationships as evidenced by the lack of relatives in the listing of friends by the widows . . . It also appears that the biological closeness of this collateral family relationship is not translated into enjoyment of association, a source of comfort in depression, a major cause of anger or the reason for feelings of importance.[10]

Families are failing to look after their widows. Yet as Christians we have a clear mandate: "If anyone does not provide for his own, and especially for those of his household, he has denied the faith, and is worse than an unbeliever" (1 Tim. 5:8).

What about our church families? Yes, they are a means of support, says Paul to Timothy, but the blood family has the primary task. "If any woman who is a believer has dependent widows, let her assist them, and let not the church be burdened, so that it may assist those who are widows indeed" (1 Tim. 5:16).

Modern society has spawned a new breed of "widows"—those women who, alone and often floundering, have suffered the separation of divorce. Bible-believing churches have been slow to encircle this forgotten—and often rejected—category of believers. To them, as to all hurting people, we need to give the words of David: "The LORD is my light and my salvation; whom shall I fear? The LORD is the defense of my life; whom shall I dread?" (Ps. 27:1).

Darkness and abandonment! These are possibly the two prospects we fear most. Darkness leaves us disoriented and isolated. Abandonment—no one looking for us or caring where we are—strips us of hope.

The frustration of loneliness is a tragedy of such magnitude that it eclipses other frustrations completely. Like cancer, it is a scourge of the modern age.[11]

In the Lord, darkness and abandonment meet His light and His salvation.

David ends Psalm 27 with confidence. He began with the affirmation of who God is — the One who dispels fear — and he concludes with strong conviction. "I would see the goodness of the LORD in the land of the living. Wait for the LORD; be strong, and let your heart take courage; yes, wait for the LORD" (Ps. 27:13,14). No matter where we put in or where we go out, the everlasting goodness of the Lord is our anchor.

On December 7, 1941, Peter Marshall, the famed chaplain of the U.S. Senate, was speaking to the cadets at Annapolis, unaware that as he spoke Pearl Harbor was in flames. Many in his audience would be called upon to give their lives in the days ahead. He told them this story.

"A young boy dying from an uncurable disease asked his mother, 'What is it like to die? Does it hurt?'

"His mother answered: 'Remember when you were a very little boy and played very hard and fell asleep on Mommy's bed? When you woke in the morning you were in your own bed because your Daddy came with his big strong arms and lifted you, undressed you, and put on your pajamas. Death is like that—you wake up in your own room.' "

10
Cleaning Up the Act Without Washing Out the Shine

On my fiftieth birthday my older sister sent me a delightfully humorous card with this message: Since most of the people in the world are under thirty-five, isn't it nice to be in the top half of something?

Middle age has been variously defined (probably according to the youth of the definer) as anywhere from forty to sixty-five years. American women who have lived at least four decades know the security of a land of personal freedom; we have tasted the fruit of affluence and unprecedented privilege. We live in lavish luxury compared to most women of the world.

When Isaiah was prophesying against the city of Jerusalem before its fall, he tongue-lashed the women: "Rise up you women who are at ease, and hear my voice; give ear to my word, you complacent daughters" (Isa. 32:9).

Like the women of Israel, we also need to hear God. With few exceptions we have been sheltered, educated, defended, cherished, and allowed to seek our own goals. Now, as Moses warned, "You may say to yourself, 'My power and the strength of my hands have produced this wealth for me.' " The place of privilege is also a place of peril, he said. "But . . . remember the LORD your God, for it is He who is giving you power to make wealth. . . . if you ever forget the LORD your God . . . you shall surely perish" (Deut. 8:18,19).

Composite Christian Wife

In the preceding pages we have looked at marriage, children, the marketplace, and self-esteem. We climbed into the ring with depression, advancing age, dangers, and death. Over it all we must write the wisdom of Proverbs:

> Trust in the LORD with all your heart, and do not lean on your own understanding. In all your ways acknowledge Him, and He will make your paths straight (Prov. 3:5,6).

How do Christian women actually feel? During 1978 and early 1979, I queried conferees from women's Bible conferences and wives of leaders who attended seminars in a half dozen cities of the United States.

The first section of my questionnaire concerned husbands. Of the forty to sixty age group, less than five in one hundred reported open distrust of their husbands. Under forty, the number rose sharply to one in ten. Of those who said their marriages were good, large segments admitted to some disappointment. In the forty to fifty age group, one-third had problems; in the fifty to sixty group nearly one-half confessed to some disappointment. Surprisingly, of those over sixty, three out of four admitted disappointment; of this group, one-third were widowed.

What areas of the marriage relationship were sore spots? By far the deepest source of distress was poor communication. One wife in every three under forty mentioned it; this number dropped steadily as the years progressed. Can it be we finally learn—or do that many drop out?

Another inflammation centered on submission. Again in later years the controversy had subsided somewhat. Surveys, however, are superficial generalizations at best; they are merely directional arrows. They tell us in what current we are swimming. Matrimonially, we need to know that the winds are blowing us far off course. Another survey, reported by *Seventeen* magazine in March, 1979, questioned a cross section of young girls (sixteen to twenty-one) concerning their marital preferences.

Forty-one percent wanted to be virgins when they were married; forty percent did not; twenty percent didn't know. Half of them knew they did *not* want their husbands to be like their fathers; less than one-third did. Two-thirds of the girls wanted a two-career family, while sixteen percent did not. Morality? More than fifty-six percent did not want to marry men who were virgins; only one in five did. And do you want to live with him before marriage? Forty-two percent said yes; thirty-nine percent said no. In all of the questions, an average of twenty percent simply did not know what they wanted.

Now, under twenty-one immaturity is obviously a big factor, but given these stated goals, marriage in the United States is far adrift from the moorings of God's design. This survey tells us, the marriage role models, something of what we must do and say. Our task is to tell wives that management of marriage belongs to God; He is the policymaker. We are to follow His rulings; He knows what He's doing. God puts a high priority on marriage. Woe to the woman who takes it for granted, or despises it, or sentimentalizes it!

Of all middle-age relationships, marriage should be the most fulfilling—like luscious fruit that is ripe, mellow, juicy, and utterly sweet. At a wedding shower I once wrote this enclosure in "Hints for Housekeeping":

> To keep husbands fresh and crisp: Do not freeze. Cold temperatures tend to break down connecting tissues in marriage. Husbands must be kept at an even dew point; they are able to maintain stability under warm circumstances, but do avoid extremes. In comfortable room temperature without too much draft they will keep indefinitely and provide long years of pleasure.

Next Generations

Motherhood—and grandmotherhood—may well be the best investment any woman can make. Training the young child monopolizes most parental manuals, but the middle years bring associations with children on adult levels. In-laws are the butt of many jokes, but the partners our children choose become our serious responsibility. In our family of four children I have often thought how complicated the lines of communication are. Each child has a connection with every other child, as well as with us, his parents. When six people relate to five others, thirty threads of interest are intertwined. Now, with each child in a marriage relationship, we touch the live ends of four new family members. New babies bring more family and more complicated communications.

I sometimes think of myself as a flow-through teabag, soaking in the warmth of sons and daughters and allowing that relationship to produce a stimulating brew that gives love and lift to family life. Looking from my vantage point, watching young people climb reminds me that I am—whether I want to be or not—an example. What a privilege! As older women pass from the scene, I become the leader of the line, the embodiment of what God wants for my daughters, my daughters-in-love, nieces, and granddaughters. What am I saying to them? God has clearly issued my orders:

> Older women likewise are to be reverent in their behavior, not malicious gossips, nor enslaved to much wine, teaching what is good . . . encourage the young women to love their husbands, to love their children, to be sensible, pure, workers at home, kind, being subject to their own husbands, that the word of God may not be dishonored (Titus 2:3–5).

Above all else that a Christian mother provides for her grown children is the shield of prayer. I looked at a mountain where rock had been quarried and watched the wind eroding it with great gusts of reddish dust. The protective layer of forest had been removed. It reminded me that prayer is the erosion-preventive for my family. Everything else I give has little value without specific intercession for each of my loved ones.

> This is the confidence which we have before Him, that, if we ask anything according to His will, He hears us. And if we know that He hears us in whatever we ask, we know that we have the requests which we have asked from Him (1 John 5:14,15).

Giving and Gabbing

Part of the fun of being older is giving gifts. Here are a few suggestions:

—Simple gifts with a personalized touch are best. Art work, macramé, needlework—any handwork is a part of yourself.

—Some of us have to trade money for other people's creations, so keep your eyes open for items to fit hobbies, reading interests, professional needs, or clothing for an upcoming event. Thinking ahead allows time for monogramming, and lets the recipient know it was not a last minute grab-bag.

—Most appreciated of all is yourself—in proper dosage. A little mom goes a long way even when you are loved dearly. Drastically ration overnight stays with married kids; hotels make visits work more smoothly.

—Most visiting is conversation—an art all of us need to cultivate constantly. Seven guards for middle-aged parents:

1. Do I belabor unimportant issues?
2. Do I put down the younger generation?
3. Do I ramble?
4. Do I overuse, or misuse, certain words or phrases?
5. Do I, in Edith Bunker style, insist on going back to the very beginning of everything?
6. Do I insist on telling jokes and stories when I'm obviously not gifted for it?
7. Am I a poor listener?

The Alert Woman

How to be an assertive (not aggressive) woman has been a popular seminar topic for a decade. Judging from publicity, assertiveness is the ability to demand a raise, to say no to lowly jobs and flirtatious men, to let all the world know you are a force to be reckoned with as you elbow your way up the corporate ladder.

Women in careers and ministries need, I believe, not so much assertiveness as alertness. The name of God's game is giving. Time, money, effort—whatever—must be given wisely. When Jesus sent His disciples out to minister, He said: "I send you out as sheep in the midst of wolves; therefore be shrewd as serpents, and innocent as doves" (Matt. 10:16).

The alert woman knows what is truly important. She is not willing to compromise eternal values. Her body, her family, her marriage, the sovereign right of God to run her life—these are nonnegotiable parts of her life.

Are you considering a job? Whether it is earning a living, volunteering time, or engaging in some phase of gospel ministry, four important questions should be asked: (1) What do I want to do? (2) What qualifies me to do it? (3) What specific contributions will I make? (4) What are my goals (and my employer's) for the next five years—ten—twenty?

"Retirement" is a loaded term, synonymous with diminished living; income, health, and lust for life are on the skids. To retire is not to quit; retirement should be a readjustment to a less-pressurized lifestyle.

One thing retirees must use is experience. Postcareer years should be the icing on the cake, a time to funnel the cream of experience into a relaxed and fulfilling occupation. A hobby of restoring furniture can become a full-time repair business. Professors and teachers regularly market their pearls on the printed page. My mother retired as a bank teller and did part-time accounting for a small business.

Several organizations—the best known is SCORE (Service Corps of Retired Executives)—are consultants for small businesses. I met a woman on a plane recently who loves clothes and works three days a week in a dress shop; her husband is the area director for the American Association of Retired Persons. One of my dearest elderly friends sells Avon cosmetics; her loving, soft-sell manner catapults her way ahead of many uptight younger women.

Making the Most of Me

I met a girl the other day
Who looked so winsome, young and gay
I studied her before and aft—
And asked: "Could that be Ethel Kraft?"
For there was something old and new
About the lady I once knew.
Her height and weight were just the same—
So was her smile, her eyes and name,
But what? I wondered, has she done
To make her sparkle like the sun?
What has occurred to change her face
And wreath it with such youthful grace?

Then dawned the truth that sparked this yarn—
She has a new roof on the barn!
A halo soft with threads of gray
Transformed my friend of yesterday.
A pretty wig had turned the trick.
And made that gal—a dashing chick. [1]

Knowing I am worth God's attention, I proceed to care for myself with confidence. It is a privilege to go to the doctor for checkups, to groom and shape up my body, to be a good steward. God made only one me.

I urge you . . . to present your bodies a living and holy sacrifice, acceptable to God, which is your spiritual service of worship. And do not be conformed to this world, but be transformed by the renewing of your mind, that you may prove what the will of God is, that which is good and acceptable and perfect (Rom. 12:1,2).

Depression? D-I-C-E

Last January, Kate of Miami, Florida, turned ninety-six. She says she has never known boredom, that life is fun. She was a first-grade school teacher, a helper with blind children, the wife of a banker, a widow, and then the marriage partner of an English literature professor. Having traveled extensively, she was asked, "What is the best place you've been?" Her answer: "The best place is where I happen to be."[2]

Optimistic satisfaction with living is the best preventive for depression. But what if the monster forces open your door, and you find yourself down, discouraged, and disgusted with the analgesic answers everybody gives? Try this four-part formula:

1. *Do some constructive physical activity.* Clean the bathroom, wash the car, rearrange books, dig up weeds, knead bread dough.

2. *Involve yourself with somebody less fortunate than you.* If you cannot visit or call someone who is sick, handicapped, or poverty-stricken, haul out the Yellow Pages and look under "Hospitals." Think of hopeless people—cripples, cardiac cases, congenitally deformed children, alcoholics, burn victims—the list is endless. Think how fortunate you are.

3. *Clean up.* Take a shower or bath—shampoo, manicure, pedicure. Put on clean clothes.

4. Energize with Ephesians. Read Ephesians 6:10–18. You will learn who is bugging you and how to fight back. Depression is mental, emotional, and spiritual. It is entirely curable and preventable—when you wear battle dress. Feelings don't think. You can't turn them off by saying to yourself, "I know I shouldn't feel like this." Whether or not you should, you already do. It's what you do with your feelings that makes the difference.

One added note:

> Research reveals that a majority of individuals who become significantly depressed feel they have no one with whom they are close. Developing a close friendship can be a first step toward becoming well.[3]

Years—Friends or Foes?

Jack Benny tickled America's funny bone with his annual birthday bulletin that he had reached thirty-nine years—and was holding. It was his way of saying that his spirit stayed young though his body was aging.

The decline and fall of the human body has long troubled man, but God commanded man to venerate age.

Have you ever . . .

—had a vague feeling that you are supposed to be someplace or do something and can't remember what?
—looked at your face in the mirror and didn't recognize it?
—found an old snapshot and started to cry?
—suddenly become nauseated at the sight of a fashion show?
—noticed a newly stiff joint?

—wondered why you had not noticed that your husband was looking stooped and "older"?

—had the urge to run away to Rio—or someplace?

Take heart; everybody does. There are a thousand little ways we find out we have indeed passed into the category of "older folks." "No! Not me!" we want to say. But we ought to say, "Wow! I'm finally getting there. Really, this newest version of me isn't too bad!"

There is an inverse ratio: as physical strength declines, moral and intellectual strength grow. Spiritual stamina deepens. "We do not lose heart, but though our outer man is decaying, yet our inner man is being renewed day by day" (2 Cor. 4:16).

When Lightning Strikes

During my years as a medical secretary, I fielded some hilarious questions. My surgeon-boss saw many patients for all kinds of head, neck, and chest ailments. The greatest enemy, I came to realize, was ignorance and fear. Do allergy injections cause hemorrhoids? I was asked—seriously. Even after surgery for a hiatal hernia, a woman paid for what she called "a high anal hernia." Anticipating repair of the delicate tympanic membrane, a man asked confidentially, "Could you tell me, is the eardrum a gristle?"

Medically sophisticated people would laugh, of course, but anxiety is very real to patients. Advancing years have somewhat the same effect. We fear them because we are ill-informed and emotionally paralyzed with fear.

A professional auto racer changed from speeding cars at six hundred miles per hour on Utah's salt flats to pulling heavy loads with tractors. He said it is an even greater sensation to compete slowly with heavy weight. That is precisely what many older people have discovered about life. Tearing around as teens, dashing through the twenties and thirties, we stumble into the frenetic forties out of breath. It's time to take a different tack. If resources are built in, a bolt of the blues at age fifty-nine cannot do much damage to a tough target. Toughness is that durability that builds with time and experience.

Professor Terman, the famous developer of the Stanford-Binet test and popularizer of the IQ test, studied a group of gifted children from all kinds of homes. One common factor ran throughout—exposure to books. The more we learn about people and places and ideas, the better equipped we are to cope with problems and challenges in our own lives.

Crises? All of us have them. An NFL coach was quoted: "Yesterday is a cancelled check, today is cash on the line, tomorrow is a promissory note. You can't fret over things you can't control."

Sin's Short Change

Not long ago I needed to mail a letter in a Florida hotel. At the stamp machine I put in my quarter, thinking I could get at least one fifteen-cent stamp, although a dime seemed an outrageous "handling fee." To my amazement and fury, out came a ten-cent stamp and four one-cent stamps! Modern lives are like that.

"OK, it's more than I should pay (for fun or some passing whim) but I'll give it a whirl," we say. So we give our effort, our bodies, our money. When our resources are gone, we discover we have been shortchanged.

CLEANING UP THE ACT

Life is pretty much gone, and death is staring us in the face. Like a mountain peak, it looms overwhelmingly large, deeply mysterious, and terribly forboding. Death, says the Bible, is the last enemy to be destroyed. But because its sentence has already been pronounced, Paul could exult: "O death, where is your victory? . . . your sting? The sting of death is sin, and the power of sin is the law; but thanks be to God, who gives us the victory through our Lord Jesus Christ (1 Cor. 15:55–57).

Everyone has to face the prospect of death. As Christians we have a living hope: "If we live, we live for the Lord, or if we die, we die for the Lord; therefore whether we live or die, we are the Lord's. . . . to live is Christ, and to die is gain" (Rom. 14:8; Phil. 1:21).

Grandma used to get teased about boning up for her finals when she read the Bible. But she was ready when God called. It has been said that no one has reached maturity until he has faced his own death and ordered his life accordingly.

Several months ago I received a letter from a young friend with terminal cancer. She included her own poem, a fitting monument to her life—and ours.

So do I fear tomorrow?
And all that may happen to me?
Or do I learn today
To live in Christ triumphantly?

Do I worry about sorrow so strong?
And say "God, please, not me"?
Or do I smile toward heaven
Knowing I'll face life victoriously?

When pain and trouble come my way
Is it more than I can bear?
Or do I raise my face toward Jesus
Knowing His love and peace He'll share?

Yes, God, you know I'm only human
But what a bad excuse.
Let me cuddle in your arms
For you are my only safe refuge.

Help me not to fear the future
Scared of what tomorrow holds
But living my life now for Jesus
Expecting that marvelous peace untold.

—-Lauri Amandus

Reflections . . .

I have asked myself why God extracted my life from that Scotch-German tuft of humanity during those lean years in the land of plenty? Why did He allow me to grow up inhaling toxic fumes from ice trucks, beer gardens, and church disputes? Why did God's infinite plan for me call for early confrontation with the Person of Jesus Christ who introduced himself to me before I had ever heard of any other historical standouts?

He made me, a girl, a woman in this place with my human connections, with mental windows and a door with the handle on the inside. He Himself stood, knocking, because He knew that when I came bursting out of my cocoon I would need Him above all others.

The world begrudges moving over to make room for me. Just a few short weeks before Pearl Harbor ushered in the era of women in industry, Sinclair Lewis spat out these words to his opponent in a debate on "Has The Modern Woman Made Good?"

A lady is a woman so incompetent as to have to take refuge in a secluded class, like kings and idiots who have to be treated with special kindness because they can't take it.

I can't help wondering what Lewis's mother would have said in response: An earlier woman, the poet Elinor Wylie, answers:

> I was, being human, born alone;
> I am, being woman, hard beset.
> I live by squeezing from a stone
> The little nourishment I can get.[4]

Man's vision is dim, able to see only what affects him the most. Jesus said: "I am the light of the world; he who follows Me shall not walk in the darkness, but shall have the light of life" (John 8:12).

A friend of mine tried again to commit suicide several weeks ago. It was after a previous attempt that she and her husband had trusted Christ as their personal Savior.

I remember when we were visiting one of their mansions and she was teaching me to play backgammon. I had the feeling it was one of her more serious pursuits in life. She is one of the "beautiful people"— the mythical idols of American women. Graceful homes, gorgeous wardrobes, wealthy, influential friends, her personal Rolls Royce—she can have whatever her heart desires. And with it all she has a loving Christian husband. What is wrong? Does Jesus Christ take away the peace He promised? Does He sometimes turn off the light? We have a dozen other friends who are seeking psychiatric counsel—or who are simply complaining of chronic fatigue and tension headaches.

I keep thinking about Peter, so excited to see the Lord walking on the water. In the boat on the Sea of Galilee they were making a nighttime crossing in choppy water. The wind kept blowing them in the wrong direction. Without sleep, and with that strained, stiff tension that builds under the fight for survival, the men saw Jesus Christ walking on the waves. It was after three in the morning; no wonder they thought they were hallucinating!

"Take courage. It is I; do not be afraid," called Jesus. Peter (speaking for me) answered huskily, "Lord, if it is you, command me to come to you on the water." More than anything he wanted to get out of that boat and be close to the calm strength and serenity of the Savior.

"Come," Christ called back. Peter vaulted the side of the boat and started out. But Peter was conditioned to be a fisherman, and he automatically kept his eye on the water. I think a big swell curled up toward him and his instinct said, "Oops, watch out!" He glanced away from the Lord and began to sink. It does not take long to go down feet first. Only a very short prayer would do: "Lord, save me!"

"Immediately Jesus stretched out His hand and took hold of him, and said to him, 'O you of little faith, why did you doubt?' " (Matt. 14:31).

Like dust settling on the furniture, fear accumulates in tiny particles. I am afraid . . . in the dark . . . I might get sick . . . I might slip on the ice . . . run out of gas . . . lose my cool . . . lose my kids . . . get lost . . . be unable to measure up. . .

When Jesus Christ was saying farewell to His disciples, He promised He would not leave them without comfort in the harsh world of anti-God reality. He said He would send a Helper—the Holy Spirit.

"[He] will teach you all things. . . . Peace I leave with you; My peace I give to you; not as the world gives, do I give to you. Let not your heart be troubled, nor let it be fearful" (John 14:26,27).

Don't be afraid. But Lord, I can't help . . . *Don't be afraid.* But you know I'm not . . . *Don't be afraid.* Lord, I try, but . . . *Do not be afraid.* All right, Lord, you're telling me fear is bad; get rid of it. Peace replaces fear. Does it just drop down magically? Do I have to do something to get it?

Isaiah answers: "The steadfast of mind Thou wilt keep in perfect peace, because he trusts in Thee" (Isa. 26:3). There's the key. My free will allows me to turn the steering wheel of my own mind. I choose to steer toward Him. I gear my personal travel route with Him in view, according to His Word. "Those who love Thy law have great peace, and nothing causes them to stumble" (Ps. 119:165).

Middle age? It's up here past the foothills. I'm like the small girl who started out straddling a shallow ditch. As I grew older, the ditch became a ravine and the banks grew farther apart. As I struggled to hang on to the tapering ledge of youth, pebbles rolled and footing became slippery. I had to cross over to the unfamiliar uphill side of aging. Over here the winds are picking up, and it's colder, but what a glorious view!

Carl Sandburg wrote: "I know a Jew fish crier down on Maxwell Street with a voice like a north wind blowing over corn stubble in January. . . . His face is that of a man terribly glad to be selling fish."[5]

I'm terribly glad to be up here holding on tightly to the Rock. "I know whom I have believed and I am convinced that He is able to guard what I have entrusted to Him until that day" (2 Tim. 1:12).

NOTES

Chapter I
1. "The Seven Problems of Aging Parents," *Good Housekeeping*, March, 1979, p. 108.
2. Philadelphia *Evening Bulletin*, July 5, 1978.
3. *Saturday Review of Literature*, April 15, 1978.

Chapter II
1. Howard J. Clinebell, Jr., *Growth Counseling For Mid-Years Couples* (Philadelphia: Fortress), p. 22. (Quoted from the Los Angeles *Times*).
2. "The Marriage Savers," *Mainliner*, February, 1977, p. 32.
3. Dr. William Appleton and Jane Appleton, *How Not To Split Up* (New York: Doubleday, 1978), pp. 9, xi, xii.
4. Lecture, July 10, 1978, Harvard Alumni College.
5. Elisabeth D. Dodds, *Marriage to a Difficult Man* (Philadelphia: Westminster, 1976), p. 11.
6. *Encyclopedia Britannica*, Vol. 13, p. 716.

Chapter III
1. M. H. Klaus *et al.*, cited by Alice S. Rossi, *Daedalus*, Spring, 1977, p. 6.
2. Philadelphia *Inquirer*, June 6, 1977.
3. Quoted by Liz Smith, *The Mother Book* (New York: Doubleday, 1978), p. 140.
4. Erma Bombeck, *If Life Is a Bowl of Cherries—What Am I Doing in the Pits?* (New York: Fawcett World, 1978), pp. 128,29.

Chapter IV
1. Dallas *Morning News*, April 14, 1979.
2. "Ambitious Timetable: CEO by 40," *American Way*, October, 1976.

3. John W. Gardner, *No Easy Victories* (New York: Harper & Row, 1968).

Chapter V
1. Autobiography, Vol. II, p. 37.
2. *Autobiography of Bertrand Russell* (Reading, Mass.: Allen & Unwin, 1975), p. 287.
3. *Faith At Work*, February, 1972, p. 13.
4. Dallas *Morning News*, April 21, 1978.
5. Jo Berry, *Can You Love Yourself?* (Glendale, Calif.: Gospel Light, 1978).
6. *Ibid.*, pp. 34,35.

Chapter VI
1. Fort Worth *Star-Telegram*, Nov. 10, 1978.
2. Nathan S. Kline, *From Sad to Glad* (New York: G. P. Putnam's Sons, 1974).
3. Percy Knauth, *Season in Hell* (New York: Harper & Row, 1975).
4. Helen Hosier, *Suicide, A Cry for Help* (Irvine, Calif.: Harvest House, 1978), p. 28.
5. Wayne E. Oates, Th.D. and Herbert Wagemaker, M.D., *Pastoral Psychology*, Vol. 25 (2), Winter, 1976, pp. 91, 92.
6. Lucy Freeman, *The Cry for Love* (New York: Macmillan, 1969).

Chapter VII
1. Gerhard Newbeck, *The Family Coordinator*, October, 1978, pp. 445–47.
2. Milton Rockmore, "Age 65 and Kicking Even Higher," *American Way*, July, 1978, pp. 25, 28.
3. *Ibid.*, p. 28.
4. David Allan Hubbard, *Beyond Futility* (Grand Rapids, Mich.: Wm. B. Eerdmans, 1976), pp. 124,25.
5. Robert and Cynthia Raines, "The Afternoon of Life," *United Presbyterian*, April, 1978, p. 30.
6. Erma Bombeck, *If Life Is a Bowl of Cherries—What Am I Doing in the Pits?* (New York: Fawcett World, 1978), pp. 231–38.

Chapter VIII
1. Bob Greene, Dallas *Morning News*, September 20, 1978.

2. David W. Ewing, "Death in the Corporate Jungle," *Saturday Review*, July 8, 1978, p. 12.
3. Dallas *Morning News*, November 22, 1973.
4. Kathy Cotton, File 13 Corporation, Inc., Bolivar, Missouri, 1972.
5. C.S. Lewis, *Christian Reflections* (Grand Rapids, Mich.: Wm. B. Eerdmans, 1967), pp. 142–51.

Chapter IX
1. "Coping With Death in the Family," *Business Week*, April 5, 1976, p. 93.
2. *Time*, June 5, 1978, p. 66.
3. Miami *Herald*, January 21, 1979.
4. *Saturday Review*, February 8, 1975, p. 8.
5. Dallas *Morning News*, December 3, 1977.
6. *Family Life*, May/June, 1978, p. 1.
7. *A Woman for All Seasons* (Nashville: Thomas Nelson, 1977).
8. Betty Jane Wylie, "Beyond the Veil," *The Canadian Province*, August 6, 1977.
9. U.S. Census Bureau, *The Family Coordinator*, October, 1978, p. 359.
10. *Journal of Marriage and Family*, May, 1978, pp. 360–362.
11. *Saturday Review*, April 3, 1976, p. 6.

Chapter X
1. Norma Alloway, *Join Us for Coffee* (Toronto: Windward, 1978), p. 165.
2. Miami *Herald*, January 21, 1979.
3. Frank B. Minirth, States V. Skipper, and Paul D. Meier, *100 Ways to Defeat Depression* (Grand Rapids, Mich.: Baker, 1979).
4. "Let No Charitable Hope," 1923.
5. "Fish Crier," 1916.